INTRODUCTION
TO
VOLUME RENDERING

ISBN 0-13-861683-3

9 780138 616830

90000

Hewlett-Packard Professional Books

Atchison	Object-Oriented Test & Management Software Development in C++
Blinn	Portable Shell Programming: An Extensive Collection of Bourne Shell Examples
Bloomers	Practical Planning for Network Growth
Caruso	Power Programming in HP OpenView: Developing CMIS Applications
Chew	The Java/C++ Cross-Reference Handbook
Cook	Building Enterprise Information Architectures
Costa	Planning and Designing High Speed Networks Using 100VG-AnyLAN, Second Edition
Crane	A Simplified Approach to Image Processing: Classical and Modern Techniques
Day	The Color Scanning Handbook: Your Guide to Hewlett-Packard ScanJet Color Scanners
Derickson	Fiber Optic Test and Measurement
Eisenmann and Eisenmann	Machinery Malfunction Diagnosis and Correction: Vibration Analysis and Troubleshooting for the Process Industries
Fernandez	Configuring the Common Desktop Environment
Fistrup	USENET: Netnews for Everyone
Fistrup	The Essential Web Surfer Survival Guide
Grady	Practical Software Metrics for Project Management and Process Improvement
Greenberg	A Methodology for Developing and Deploying Internet and Intranet Solutions
Grosvenor, Ichiro, O'Brien	Mainframe Downsizing to Upsize Your Business: IT-Preneuring
Gunn	A Guide to NetWare® for UNIX®
Helsel	Graphical Programming: A Tutorial for HP VEE
Helsel	Visual Programming with HP VEE, Second Edition
Holman, Lund	Instant JavaScript
Kane	PA-RISC 2.0 Architecture
Knouse	Practical DCE Programming
Lee	The ISDN Consultant: A Stress-Free Guide to High-Speed Communications
Lewis	The Art & Science of Smalltalk
Lichtenbelt, Crane, Naqvi	Introduction to Volume Rendering
Loomis	Object Databases in Practice
Lund	Integrating UNIX® and PC Network Operating Systems
Madell	Disk and File Management Tasks on HP-UX
Mahoney	High-Mix Low-Volume Manufacturing
Malan, Letsinger, Coleman	Object-Oriented Development at Work: Fusion In the Real World
McFarland	X Windows on the World: Developing Internationalized Software with X, Motif® and CDE
McMinds/Whitty	Writing Your Own OSF/Motif Widgets
Norton, DiPasquale	Thread Time: The Multithreaded Programming Guide
Orzessek, Sommer	ATM: & MPEG-2: A Practical Guide to Computer Security
Phaal	LAN Traffic Management
Pipkin	Halting the Hacker: A Practical Guide to Computer Security
Poniatowski	The HP-UX System Administrator's "How To" Book
Poniatowski	HP-UX 10.x System Administration "How To" Book
Poniatowski	Learning the HP-UX Operating System
Poniatowski	The Windows NT and HP-UX System Administrator's How To Book
Poniatowski	The HP-UX System Administration Handbook and Toolkit
Ryan	Distributed Object Technology: Concepts and Applications
Simmons	Software Measurement: A Visualization Toolkit
Thomas	Cable Television Proof-of-Performance: A Practical Guide to Cable TV Compliance Measurements Using a Spectrum Analyzer
Weygant	Clusters for High Availability: A Primer of HP-UX Solutions
Witte	Electronic Test Instruments
Yawn, Stachnick, Sellars	The Legacy Continues: Using the HP 3000 with HP-UX and Windows NT

Introduction to Volume Rendering

Barthold Lichtenbelt
Randy Crane
Shaz Naqvi

Hewlett-Packard Company

Prentice Hall PTR
Upper Saddle River, NJ 07458
www.phptr.com

Library of Congress Cataloging-in-Publication Data

Lichtenbelt, Barthold.
    Introduction to volume rendering / Barthold Lichtenbelt, Randy
Crane, Shaz Naqvi : Hewlett-Packard Company.
        p.   cm. — (Hewlett-Packard professional books)
    Includes bibliographical references and index.
    ISBN 0–13–861683–3
    1. Computer graphics.   2. Three-dimensional display systems.
I. Crane, Randy.   II. Naqvi, Shaz.   III. Hewlett-Packard Company.
IV. Title.   V. Series.
T385.L53   1998
006.6'93—dc21   98–12074
                                                    CIP

Editorial/production supervision: Nicholas Radhuber
Manufacturing manager: Alan Fischer
Acquisitions editor: John Anderson
Marketing manager: Dan Rush
Cover design: Anthony Gemmellaro
Cover design director: Jerry Votta
Manager, Hewlett-Packard Press: Patricia Pekary

Published by Prentice Hall PTR
Prentice-Hall, Inc.
A Simon & Schuster Company
Upper Saddle River, New Jersey 07458

Prentice Hall books are widely used by corporations and government agencies
for training, marketing, and resale.

The publisher offers discounts on this book when ordered in bulk quantities.
For more information, contact:
Phone: 800-382-3419
Fax: 201-236-7141; e-mail: corpsales@prenhall.com
or write:
Prentice Hall PTR
Corporate Sales Department
One Lake St.
Upper Saddle River, NJ 07458

All product names mentioned herein are the trademarks of their respective owners.

Printed in the United States of America
10 9 8 7 6 5 4 3 2 1

ISBN 0-13-861683-3

Prentice-Hall International (UK) Limited, *London*
Prentice-Hall of Australia Pty. Limited, *Sydney*
Prentice-Hall Canada Inc., *Toronto*
Prentice-Hall Hispanoamericana, S.A., *Mexico*
Prentice-Hall of India Private Limited, *New Delhi*
Prentice-Hall of Japan, Inc., *Tokyo*
Simon & Schuster Asia Pte. Ltd., *Singapore*
Editora Prentice-Hall do Brasil, Ltda., *Rio de Janeiro*

CONTENTS

PREFACE

The popularity of volume rendering has grown considerably these last few years. Due to the increase in desktop computing power, volume rendering has become more accessible to more people. For years, volume rendering applications were found almost solely in medical imaging. Now, volume rendering is used in diverse applications such as fluid dynamics, meteorology, failure analysis, and molecular modeling. The list of applications grows everyday.

This book is for everyone who would like to explore volume rendering and its uses. Those professionals who regularly inspect three-dimensional sampled data will benefit greatly from the concepts presented in this book. This book will aid students of computer science and engineering who wish to know the best way to interactively view three-dimensional sampled data sets. Anyone interested in volume rendering concepts such as classification, lighting, ray casting, and compositing will find this book useful.

If you are interested in volume rendering, there are two compelling reasons to own this book.

First, it is a comprehensive introduction to all the concepts you need to understand in order to volume render. Previously, the method of gathering all that information required a pile of IEEE transactions, a copy machine, and reams of paper. We have already done that and are anxious to pass the savings on to you.

While reading all those transactions, we processed them for you. No obscure Greek letters are present, unless it is essential to the discussion. We culled the pertinent discussions while leaving the irrelevant information behind. We also augmented those discussions with our own experience. What we present to you is an organized, understandable, logical progression through the volume rendering pipeline.

Second, we strongly believe that a great part of the learning process requires hands-on experience. For this reason, a CD-ROM comes with the book. The CD-ROM includes source code, executable programs, and data sets to use. This gives you full control over your own volume renderer. You can perform unlimited "what if" experiments. If you wish to alter the order of the operations in the pipeline, or modify the gradient function, or maybe even add another light source, you can do it. With each successive experiment, you will get a better understanding of volume rendering.

Since this book cannot cover the esoteric aspects of volume rendering in great detail, we include a generous bibliography. Each chapter contains a section titled For Further Study which refers to the pertinent works in the reference section.

The first chapter of this book opens with an introduction to volume rendering. We explain exactly what volume rendering is and is not. Some volume rendering applications are presented next. Since new applications appear daily, we are only able to scratch the surface. You may wonder where to get 3-D data to manipulate. The next section in Chapter 1 covers volume acquisition, representation, and storage. An introduction of the volume rendering pipeline rounds out this chapter. This pipeline will be the basis of the presentations in the rest of the book.

The second chapter presents the framework for a basic volume renderer. As we go through the book, we will build upon this framework. This framework, as presented, will perform a simple maximum intensity projection. Chapter 2 also covers the concepts of three-dimensional transformation and projection. We follow the OpenGL model of viewing objects and extend this to volume data sets. This discussion will serve as the centerpiece of the basic volume rendering framework.

The next four chapters ("Illumination and Shading," "Classification," "Interpolation," and "Compositing") will take you step by step through the volume rendering pipeline. Each chapter presents a number of algorithms available for use in that particular block. As with any algorithm, these algorithms all have certain trade-offs that must be weighed when implementing your volume renderer.

Chapter 7 talks of volume slicing. It includes a discussion of multiplanar reformatting.

Chapter 8 is dedicated to the trade-offs that must be addressed when implementing your volume renderer. The specific topics we address are rendering performance of a complete volume visualization system, quality, precision, and optimizations.

This book is both a course and a resource guide. The main section of the book presents the methods of volume rendering. The appendices provide helpful resources for anyone involved in volume rendering. These resources include related periodicals, volume data sets and source code, and volume visualization organizations and conferences. Also included is a list of other software products to analyze. We have also included the Voxelator volume rendering extensions to the OpenGL API. The Voxelator is an API (Application Program Interface) that sets a standard for a volume rendering pipeline as presented in detail in this book.

The information in this book comes from many different sources: books, articles, courses, and so on. It should prove to be a valuable reference manual. Prior to this publication, those who were interested in volume rendering relied on their filing system full of different volume rendering papers. We hope that this book will replace that filing system. Your best resource is the index at the back of this book.

The code on the CD-ROM is C and was developed in the Win32 environment of both Windows NT and Windows 95. We developed it using Microsoft's Visual C++ compiler. Much of the code is portable to other platforms.

In the past, interactive volume rendering was used exclusively by those with access to supercomputer capabilities. The dramatic improvements in CPU power have brought interactive volume rendering to the desktop. As more ingenious ways are invented to scan objects in three dimensions, volume rendering will be used in even more applications. We hope that this book removes some of the complexities of volume rendering and that with this new understanding, you will apply volume rendering to your own new application.

Barthold Lichtenbelt (barthold@verinet.com)
Randy Crane
Shaz Naqvi

ACKNOWLEDGMENTS

The initial idea of writing this book came about at SIGGRAPH 1996. It was there that we realized how many people were interested in volume rendering. To those people who encouraged us directly and indirectly, we are thankful.

We had many individuals help us in the production of the book. John Clyne of the National Center for Atmospheric Research was indeed instrumental. He provided not only many images but also generously shared with us his years of expertise visualizing all types of data sets.

Many images were not generated by us but were generously donated from internal and external Hewlett-Packard sources. We are indebted to John Clyne, Jennifer Moyer, Christof Reinhart, Hanspeter Pfister, Tom Malzbender, Craig Wittenbrink, Mike Goss, Prof. K. H. Hoehne, and Randi Rost for the images donated.

Several images used in this book were rendered from data sets that can be found in the University of North Carolina at *Chapel Hill Volume Rendering Test Data Set*, Volume 1. We have used the head data, a 109-slice MRI data set of a human head, and the HIPIB data, the result of a quantum mechanical calculation of SOD data of a one-electron orbital of HIPIP, an iron protein. The head data is shown in Figures 2.14 and 4.8. The HIPIP is shown in Figure 4.7.

The lobster data set in Figure 2.11 is courtesy of Bob Mazaika of Advanced Visual Systems, via Mark Kessler, University of Michigan Medical School. This data set is on the CD-ROM. The data set used to render the images in Figure 3.7 is courtesy of the Mayo Clinic, and can also be found on the CD-ROM. The data set used to render Figure 4.5 is courtesy of Landmark Graphics and is provided to us by Srinivas Manapragada. This data set can be found on the CD-ROM. The images in Figure 4.10 were rendered by Christof Reinhart, Volume Graphics, GmbH, and the data set supplied by Mr. Schillinger from the TU Munich. Ramani Pichumani, Stanford University School of Medicine, donated the data set that was used to render Figure 6.7. This data set is also on the CD-ROM. Allen Anderson, Medical Imaging Research Laboratory, Department of Radiology, University of Utah, gave us the data set we used to render Figure 6.8. The trabecular bone data set on the CD-ROM was donated by Tony Keaveny from the Berkeley Orthopaedic Biomechanics Laboratory. Craig Wittenbrink and Andy Hsia were very helpful in getting the data set to us.

Input was sought from technical luminaries in the field. We appreciate those who reviewed the manuscript and provided copious suggestions. These people include Tom Malzbender, Hanspeter Pfister, Kartik Subbarao, and John C. Russ. Jeff Burrell's expertise and knowledge of medical imaging devices, and MRI scanners in particular, were thankfully drawn upon.

This work would not be possible without support of Hewlett-Packard and our immediate managers. Ken Severson and Amanda Wright were especially supportive and ensured that we had the resources needed.

Last but not least, thanks go out to our families, especially Gabi, Becky, and Janine, who supported us in our absence while we wrote, illustrated, and programmed into the wee hours of the morning.

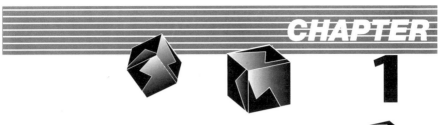

INTRODUCTION

WHAT IS VOLUME RENDERING?

Simply put, volume rendering is a method of displaying volumetric data as a two-dimensional image. The volume data may be the result of sampling an object in three dimensions. One example of this would be a magnetic resonance image (MRI) scan of a person's head. Through volume rendering, this set of samples in three dimensions can be transformed into a meaningful image viewed in two dimensions on your computer screen.

Some disciplines that share common functions with volume rendering include computer graphics and image processing. Though they share common concepts, these disciplines are different.

Traditional computer graphics simulate a scene from basic building blocks called primitives. Primitives include lines, points, and polygons. These primitives can be combined in arbitrary sizes, colors, and orientations to synthesize a scene. Texture can be added to the objects by a process called texture mapping to add realism. The addition of lighting to the scene adds even more realism. The action of "painting" these pictures on a computer screen is called rendering. An example of a rendered scene is shown in Figure 1.1(a).

Though strikingly realistic scenes can be achieved with computer graphics, if you want to look beyond the object surfaces into the object, you will find nothing. These scenes lack the internal matter that you would find in objects in the real world. It is very hard to combine the computer graphics primitives mentioned above to truthfully represent the inside of an object as well, like the inside of a human body. This is where volume rendering comes into play. We will show later that the ability to render the inside of objects is one of the advantages of volume rendering.

Image processing is the science of manipulating an image. Manipulations include enhancing the image via sharpening, isolating specific features of the image via filtering, or compositing an image from two separate images. Figure 1.1(b) shows the results of inverting the intensity values of a rectangular portion of the image.

This book is about volume rendering. Volume rendering operates on three-dimensional data, processes it, and transforms it into a simple two-dimensional image. Figure 1.1(c) shows a two-dimensional representation of a three-dimensional heart data set, rendered using volume rendering.

a

FIGURE 1.1   (a) Computer graphics; (b) processed image; (c) volume rendered heart. (Image courtesy of Volume Graphics, GmbH, Germany.)

b

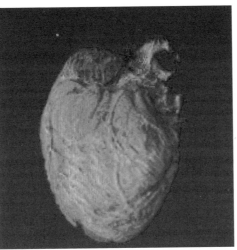

c

FIGURE 1.1 *Continued*

In the rendering process, volume rendering uses lighting functions from the study of computer graphics. It uses point processing from image processing to classify its data. In its compositing function, it emulates an alpha blend from computer graphics. Alpha blending is also in the family of frame processes in image processing.

The idea behind volume rendering is to create a two-dimensional image that is composed of numerous three-dimensional values. An example of volume rendering is an X-ray machine (see Figure 1.2). The actual output of an X-ray machine is a two-dimensional image. This image represents three-dimensional data, in this case a human body. As X-rays are passed through the body, one of three things can happen. The X-rays can penetrate without interaction, or they can be completely absorbed. Lastly, they can interact and be deflected from their original direction. On the other side of the body, the energy from these X-rays is recorded on film. This two-dimensional film represents a three-dimensional body.

You will soon see that the process of volume rendering is very similar to this X-ray machine (see Figure 1.3). Imaginary rays are passed through a three-dimensional object. As the rays travel through the data, they take into account the intensity of each datum and each ray keeps an accumulated value. As the rays leave the data, they comprise a sheet of accumulated values. These values represent the volumetric data projected onto a two-dimensional space. Through a process called classification, certain data points of

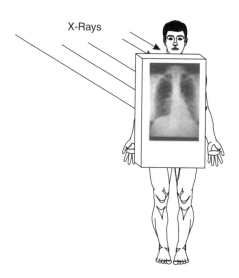

FIGURE 1.2   X-Ray machine.

FIGURE 1.3 (a) Passing imaginary rays through head; (b) head rendered on computer screen.

the three-dimensional object can be made transparent. This allows the features of interest to be viewed more easily.

VOLUME RENDERING APPLICATIONS

There are many different disciplines and sciences that work with and process three-dimensional data routinely. We will discuss several of them in this section and will show why they benefit from using volume rendering.

Medical Imaging

Medical imaging was one of the first applications of volume rendering. In the case of human internals captured with MRI and CT scanners, physicians needed ways to not only rotate, zoom, and view this three-dimensional data, but also to color it properly to distinguish one type of tissue from another. Volume rendering does that as well as make some tissues transparent so the physician can focus on the other features of interest without their being blocked by the irrelevant tissues.

Ultrasound, PET, and SPECT scanners produce huge amounts of data daily for doctors to analyze. With this data, doctors can monitor the growth of an unborn child, or find malignant tumors, blood clots, or other harmful formations.

One of the newer applications of volume rendering in medical imaging is surgical planning. By viewing the sampled data merged with synthetic surgery tools, like scalpels, on a computer screen, a doctor can proceed step by step through an operation beforehand without involving the patient. This preoperation exercise may expose possible problems that can be anticipated before the patient is opened up.

Another new application is the merger of volume rendering with haptics and telepresence surgery. Haptics is the term used for a system that generates touch feedback to the user of this system. The combination of these technologies allows a doctor to conduct surgery on a patient in a remote location. The doctor, using haptic tools with physical touch feedback, goes through the motions of an operation. The physical location and movement of the tools are transmitted to a robot at the site of the actual operation. The robot mimics the doctor's movements with actual surgical instruments.

Paleontology

Dinosaur seekers are using volume rendering while digging up fossils. Volume rendering aids paleontologists to discern between a fossil and the earth that encompasses it. The process includes scanning a chunk of earth with a CT scanner. Given the exact location of the specimen in the chunk, scientists are able to extract the fossils without destroying them. Paleontologists can also view and study the internal structure of dinosaur eggs, of which there are fewer than 200.

Jack Horner, a well-known paleontologist and curator at the Museum of the Rockies, began using three-dimensional imaging technology in 1993. He predicts that CT scanning and three-dimensional imaging will play an increasing role in paleontology in the next 20 years. Figure 1.4 and Plate 1 shows an example of visualizing a dinosaur egg.

FIGURE 1.4 Rendering of a dinosaur egg. (Image courtesy of Jennifer Moyer, Hewlett-Packard Company.)

Computational Fluid Dynamics

Fluid dynamics is the study of fluid flow. This science is the basis of air conditioning and heating system designs. Fluid dynamics is used heavily in designing intake and exhaust manifolds for engines. It is used to analyze air flow over an airplane wing and through a hair dryer. It has even been used to analyze things as esoteric as ski jumping styles. Figure 1.5 and Plate 2 shows one frame of a simulation of the development of a fire.

Fluid flow is governed by a set of differential equations known as the Navier-Stokes equations. From these equations, the velocity and vorticity of fluid flow can be derived. Vorticity, the rotational nature of flow, is a vector quantity consisting of three components at each point in space. Monitoring all of these values through a structure can be very difficult. Scientists are using volume rendering

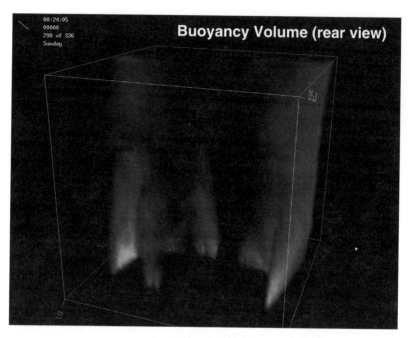

FIGURE 1.5 Single frame of a model of fire development. (Image courtesy of the National Center for Atmospheric Research, Boulder, Colorado.)

technology to view these values in three dimensions. By visualizing these values, they can quickly find regions of high vorticity and gain an overall feel for the flow through an entire system.

Modeling

Computational fluid dynamics is just one example of modeling systems. Many different systems are modeled and viewed using volume rendering techniques. At the National Center for Atmospheric Research in Boulder, Colorado, they model different phenomena like ocean turbulence, precipitation, solar magnetic storms, the ozone layer, acid rain, hurricanes, and typhoons. Figure 1.6 and Plate 3 shows how cloud development around the planet can be modeled.

We will see in the future that as computational power increases, volume rendering will be used more and more to view complex models.

FIGURE 1.6   Model of cloud development. (Image courtesy of the National Center for Atmospheric Research, Boulder, Colorado.)

Education

Today school children can view the innards of a frog without the distasteful task of dissection. Volume rendering provides a method for viewing the insides of something without having to physically remove layers.

One example of this is the visible human project. This project was spearheaded by the National Library of Medicine and cost over $1.4 million. The purpose was to create a digital image data set of complete male and female cadavers in CT, MRI, and anatomical modes.

The male CT data consists of axial CT scans at 1-mm intervals. These frames are sampled at 12-bit gray scale. Sagittal and Coronal images have been reconstructed from the axial scan.

The male MRI images are 12-bit gray scale at 256 by 256 pixels. The images are axial and coronal samples taken at 4-mm and 5-mm intervals, depending on which part of the body was being sampled.

The anatomical mode consists of 24-bit color photographs of axial cross sections at 1-mm intervals. The female cadaver was sectioned every 0.33 mm. Figure 1.7 shows how the cadaver was milled for the anatomical photographs. In order to get the anatomical photographs the cadavers had to be physically destroyed layer by layer.

The initial aim was for this data to be used in clinical medicine and biomedical research, but it is finding its way into other applications. Many educational packages on the market are using the visible human data set.

Volume rendering of the visible human is only one example of volume rendering in education (see Figure 1.8). As more and more data sets of different objects become available, you may see volume rendering of machinery in a mechanical engineering course, or in a dentistry class where you might monitor the progress of tooth decay.

FIGURE 1.7   Milling of the visible male. (Photo courtesy of the National Center for Atmospheric Research, Boulder, Colorado.)

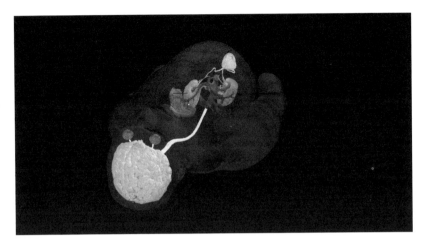

FIGURE 1.8   A rendering of the visible human highlighting internal organs. (Image courtesy of the National Center for Atmospheric Research, Boulder, Colorado.)

Nondestructive Testing

In 1926, the German Physicist Werner Heisenberg concluded that it was impossible to measure the trajectory of an electron moving through space. The very act of observing the electron altered its path and contaminated the experiment. From this phenomenon came the famous uncertainty principle.

Failure analysts run into this principle every day. An example is studying a failing integrated circuit. To view the die of the faulty chip you have to remove the package. This is typically done by grinding it off. When you finally reach the die, how do you determine the effects of the grinding? If you find a stress fracture on the die, how do you know if it was there before the die was "tampered" with?

In instances where you need to study the inner structure of something without destroying it, volume rendering can help. Industrial CT scans of engine blocks and turbines have captured the data necessary to reconstruct images of the inner structure, allowing mechanical and materials engineers to find stress fractures and other structural flaws without dissembling the object. Figure 1.9 shows a volume rendering of an industrial CT scan of a lock.

FIGURE 1.9 Internals of a magnetic lock. (Image courtesy of Volume Graphics, GmbH, Germany.)

Microscopic Analysis

For decades microbiologists and other users of microscopes had to force everything that they wanted to analyze between two glass slides. Since most objects they want to analyze are three dimensional, that severely limited their possibilities, until Laser Scan Confocal Microscopes (LSCM) became a practical alternative.

With the confocal microscope, it is possible to get high-resolution optical slices of a microscopic object without having to disturb the specimen. This is done by optically sampling a sequence of two-dimensional planes that are later combined into a three-dimensional point-sampled array.

Once the three-dimensional data is captured, the scientists can use volume rendering to scale, rotate, zoom, and display the objects for study (see Figure 1.10; Plate 4). They can also "peel" off outer layers of the object to get to the features of interest.

Though microbiologists were the first to benefit from confocal microscopy, others, seeing the benefits, were quick to jump on the bandwagon. Materials engineers use it to study fractures and other imperfections in various substances. Scientists use it to analyze the structure of silver halide grains in photographic emulsion, measure the thickness of the coating of a time release capsule, or study the pores of plastics.

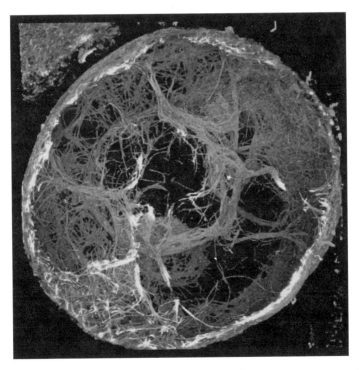

FIGURE 1.10   Stage 1 frog ocyte rendered from more than 50 contiguous optical sections. (Image courtesy of VayTek Inc.)

Oil Exploration

Volume rendering allows geoscientists to visualize such geological information as rock porosity, pressure, temperature, and permeability. This is done by sampling seismic data miles below the surface, and then volume rendering it (see Figure 1.11). With this information, geophysicists can locate promising fields for petroleum accumulations.

Deciding where best to drill an oil well depends on several factors. The first is an analysis of the seismic structure that may contain

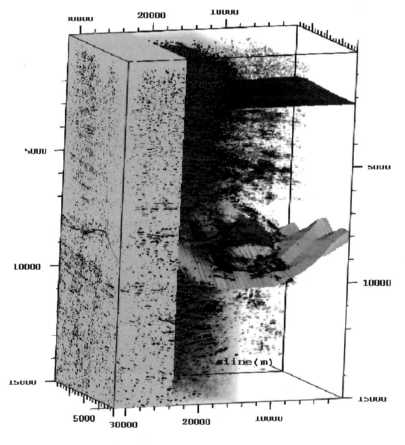

FIGURE 1.11   Annotated earth sample. (Image courtesy of CogniSeis Development.)

oil. A good prospect is an inverted bowl indicating a possible location of oil or water. The next factor to consider is the rate of change in the seismic structure. If it is consistent with the model for a structure containing oil, it is a good candidate.

Currently, the majority of oil wells drilled are "dry." It has been predicted that by using volume rendering techniques to analyze subsurface structures, hit rates as high as 80 percent could be achieved. This has the potential of saving billions of dollars for petroleum companies.

Future Applications

The number of volume rendering applications is limited only by our thinking and current sampling techniques. As sampling technology advances and we have data that represents the internals of more dissimilar objects, the number of volume rendering applications will increase. Perhaps there will be a day when miners use volume rendering to find diamonds or gold. The common plumber may use volume rendering to find exactly where pipes are stopped up. Computer games programmers searching for the ultimate realistic photo effect may render actual human "guts" in their latest shoot-em-up offering. There may even come a day when Hostess™ uses volume rendering to monitor its Twinkie filling process.

VOLUME ACQUISITION

A digital image consists of a two-dimensional array of data elements representing color or simple light intensity. These data elements are referred to as pixels, short for picture elements.

In the same manner a volume can be represented with a three-dimensional array of values. These values are called voxels, short for volume elements (see Figure 1.12). In the literature you will find two different definitions for voxels. One definition considers a voxel to be a small cube with some small size; the other considers a voxel a point without a size in three-dimensional space. We will use the second definition.

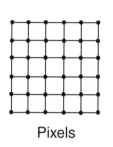
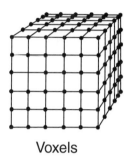

Pixels   Voxels

FIGURE 1.12   Pixels vs. voxels.

In this book, the term *voxels* will refer to the original sampled data set. Once these data points are resampled via an interpolation method, they will be referred to as *samples*.

At the beginning of this chapter we said that there are several primitives, like points and lines, used in conventional computer graphics to build a scene. A voxel is nothing more than another primitive that can be used to render a scene. In computer graphics you can think of using voxels as yet another tool to render an image the way you want it to help you visualize a scene.

Sampling and Quantizing

Sampling is the act of measuring a physical property at a specific location. The property may be light intensity, hue, density, temperature, acceleration, and so on. The locations are usually, but not, always confined to specific regular spacing on a rectangular grid. The spacing of the samples taken is referred to as the spatial resolution. Figure 1.13 compares different spatial resolutions of a two-dimensional image.

Quantizing is the process of converting a sample into digital form. The number of bits used to store the converted sample is called the intensity resolution. The higher the number of bits, the higher the intensity resolution. Figure 1.14 shows the same two-dimensional image with different intensity resolutions.

Figure 1.13 Example of different spatial resolutions: (a) 512×512; (b) 128×128; (c) 64×64; (d) 32×32; (e) 16×16.

Figure 1.14 Example of different intensity resolutions: (a) 8 bits/pixel; (b) 6 bits/pixel; (c) 4 bits/pixel; (d) 2 bits/pixel; (e) 1 bit/pixel.

ACQUISITION TECHNIQUES

So far we have described where volume rendering can be used, and what the difference between pixels and voxels is. In this section we will discuss some of the more common ways of collecting a set of voxels, commonly called a data set.

Magnetic Resonance Imaging

In 1952, Felix Bloch and Edward Purcell received the Nobel Prize in physics for their pioneering work in nuclear magnetic resonance. The application of their findings to imaging did not occur until the 1970s.

Magnetic Resonance Imaging (MRI) has a distinct advantage over other medical imaging methods. It can selectively image different tissue characteristics. Because of this, MRI is the most complex method of the three medical imaging modalities discussed here.

One of the most impressive things about an MRI scanner is the huge magnetic coils that produce magnetic fields with magnitudes of several tesla. Figure 1.15 shows an MRI scanner. When a patient

FIGURE 1.15   MRI scanner. (Photo courtesy of Elscint, Inc.)

is placed in this strong magnetic field, the hydrogen atom nuclei in the tissues align with this strong magnetic field. During this alignment process, the nuclei tend to vacillate about the magnetic field. This resonant oscillation is known as the magnetic resonance phenomenon.

Though the large magnet is the most prominent element of an MRI scanner, it is only one of the vital components. There are two sets of coils that complete the necessary elements of an MRI scanner: gradient coils and radio frequency (RF) coils. The gradient coils are used to inject an out-of-phase excitation pulse to perturb the aligned atoms away from the main magnetic field. As these atoms realign with the main field, they transmit energy back to the RF coils. Since different tissues have dissimilar hydrogen atom densities, they release energy at different levels. Higher densities release more energy. This energy variance is what creates a dynamic range of values in the final image.

The excitation pulse applied consists of unique gradient profiles. These gradient profiles are other magnetic fields typically several thousand times weaker than the main magnetic field. They are generated by separate sets of coils. Each profile is unique and referred to as x-, y-, or z-gradients (see Figure 1.16). Shortly after the excitation pulse is applied into the body, the resonating tissues transmit these signals back to the RF coils. The coils act as antennae to capture these signals. The signals are measured and then stored digitally.

During the data recording process, different body slices have distinctive frequency and phase characteristics so that the slice data can be isolated during image reconstruction. The acquisition phase usually consists of several passes over the patient's body. When all the samples are acquired, the different frequency components are summed in the time domain and translated back into the spatial domain via a Fourier transform. Although not commonly done, reconstruction of the image is also possible with a technique called filtered back projection. This technique is explained in a later section on computed tomography.

An MRI image is a map of RF intensities emitted by tissues. The brighter a particular area, the greater the signal intensity at that point. Dark areas in an image indicate where no signals are produced.

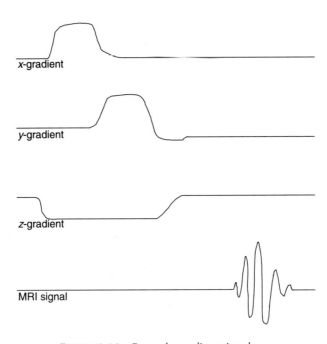

x-gradient

y-gradient

z-gradient

MRI signal

FIGURE 1.16 Example gradient signals.

The complexity of MRI makes it a very powerful imaging tool. With spatial and amplitude control over the gradients, technicians can program unique profiles to isolate arbitrary planes of data. Specific tissue characteristics can also be isolated, allowing technicians and physicians to identify tumor or tissue inflammation. An obvious advantage MRI has over CT scanners is the absence of ionizing radiation.

Ultrasound

Ultrasound is commonly used to view a fetus so that any health problems can be detected and perhaps even to determine its sex before birth. Due to its ability to produce images of flowing blood through the vascular system, ultrasound is also especially useful when imaging the heart and vasculature. Figure 1.17 shows an ultrasound monitor in operation.

FIGURE 1.17 Ultrasound monitor. (Photo courtesy of Hewlett-Packard Company.)

An ultrasound imaging system uses frequencies in the range from 1 megahertz to 20 megahertz. This high-frequency sound interacts with structures within the human body and the resulting echoes can be used to create images.

Medical technicians don't just bombard the body with waves of ultrasound. It is an exact science. Well-defined highly calibrated beams pass over the body. The sound is emitted in pulses through the body, rather than as a continuous stream of vibration. The pulses occur at a rate of about 1,000 per second. Pulsing the ultrasound makes it easier to monitor the reflected echo pulses.

The source of echoes is the boundary between different tissues. The amplitude of the returning echo is determined by how much the two tissues differ in terms of acoustic impedance. For example, at boundaries between soft tissue and bone, strong reflection pulses are produced.

As ultrasound pulses move through matter, they can be absorbed or reflected. At most tissue boundaries, only a portion of the pulse is reflected. It is divided into two pulses: a reflection pulse and the original pulse. The original pulse continues to penetrate other material. This is shown in Figure 1.18.

The location of the boundary in the horizontal and vertical direction is determined by the location of the beam. The depth is determined by the time required for the echo pulse to return. With the spatial coordinates, pulse amplitude, and return time, it is relatively easy to reconstruct a three-dimensional image. The image is a map showing the locations of echo-producing sites. Figure 1.19 and Plate 5 shows rendered ultrasound data.

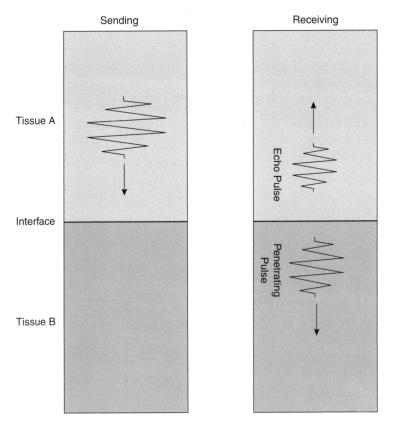

FIGURE 1.18 Echo and penetrating pulses of ultrasound.

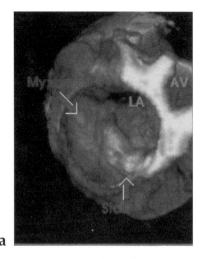 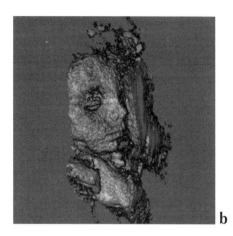

a   b

FIGURE 1.19   (a) Left atrial myxoma. (Photo courtesy of Hewlett-Packard; image rendered by TomTec Imaging Systems.) (b) Fetus. (Photo courtesy of VayTek Inc.)

Computed Tomography

Computed tomography acquires slices of a three-dimensional object. The two-dimensional slices are then aligned to create a three-dimensional data set. The acquisition consists of projecting X-rays through a slice of the body. The radiation that penetrates the body is measured by an array of detectors on the other side of the body. The detectors do not see the entire body profile, only the intensity of the beam at that particular orientation.

In order to create an entire profile of the body slice, many measurements must be taken. The X-ray tube is rotated, more beams are projected, and the intensities measured. Typically, several hundred views are taken with the results being stored in a computer.

The CT scanner has an X-ray tube mounted on a circular gantry. The tube is then able to rotate around the patient's body. There are two types of detector configurations. One type of scanner rotates a segment of detectors around the body opposite the X-ray tube. This arrangement is shown in Figure 1.20.

A second type of scanner has a full ring of stationary detectors that record measurements as the X-ray tube rotates. Figure 1.21 shows this configuration.

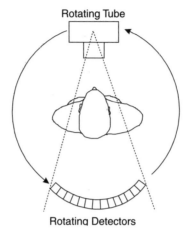

FIGURE 1.20   CT scanner with rotating detectors.

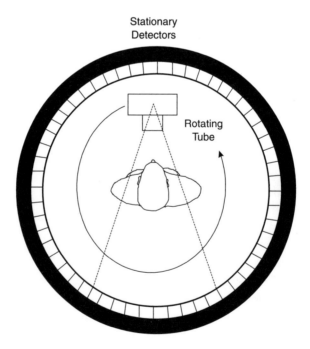

FIGURE 1.21   CT scanner with stationary detectors.

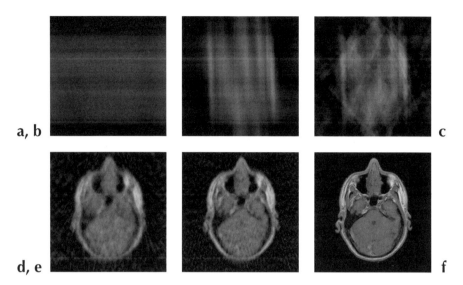

a, b

c

d, e

f

FIGURE 1.22   Reconstruction of an image slice via filtered back projection: (a) result of 1 projection; (b) result of 2 projections; (c) result of 4 projections; (d) result of 16 projections; (e) result of 32 projections; (f) final image.

The scanning is only the first part of the data slice generation. The slice must now be reconstructed from these numerous measurements. The reconstruction process employs a technique called filtered back projection. This technique, in principle, is the inverse of the scanning process. The reconstruction is possible by projecting the sampled intensities back onto some image area. Figure 1.22 shows a simple example of this. The example shows up to 32 projected samples. Typically, several hundred samples are used to reconstruct one slice.

A set of reconstructed slices can be stacked to create a three-dimensional data set.

Confocal Microscopy

Earlier in this chapter we discussed how three-dimensional data from a confocal microscope can be volume rendered. This section describes how a confocal microscope works and collects three-dimensional data.

In 1957, Marvin Minsky applied for a patent for a microscope that was radically different than microscopes at that time. His microscope used a staged-scanning confocal optical system. His idea was very farsighted. It wasn't until the 1980s that this instrument was offered commercially.

In a confocal microscope, the traditional microscope condenser is replaced by a lens just like the objective lens. A pinhole positioned on the microscope axis limits the field of illumination. The new "condenser" projects a reduced image of the pinhole onto the specimen. A second, or exit, pinhole in the image plane also restricts the field of view. Figure 1.23 shows how this works.

By moving the specimen, it can be scanned through a point of light. The photoelectric cell measures the amount of light modulated by the specimen that passes through the second pinhole. This second pinhole rejects all light scattered from all other parts. The resulting image has eliminated all objects that don't lie in the exact plane of focus.

The focus plane is stepped through the specimen to acquire a series of two-dimensional slices. The slices are stacked to build a three-dimensional data set representing the microscopic volume.

Today's confocal microscopes implement much more advanced optical paths than Minsky's original patent. Most of the designs include an elaborate assembly of mirrors and partial mirrors, called dichroic mirrors, that separate incident and reflected light. Figure 1.24 shows a confocal laser scanning microscope available today.

Fluorescent dyes are often used with confocal microscopy. These dyes adhere to certain proteins and fluoresce when exposed

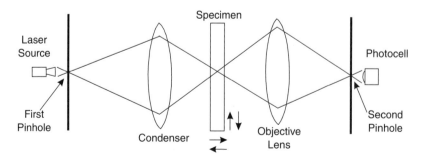

FIGURE 1.23 How a confocal microscope works.

FIGURE 1.24   The Oz confocal laser scanning microscope. (Photo courtesy of NORAN Instruments Inc.)

to ultraviolet light. This fluorescence aids in the location of struc-tures that are smaller than a wavelength of light. This combination can be used to take the place of an electron microscope. The added benefit is that it does not require killing the specimen under study.

The advantages of a confocal microscope over a traditional mi-croscope are many. The greatest ones include reduced blurring from light scattering, increased effective resolution, and inclusion of depth information.

Industrial Scanners

There are a number of three-dimensional scanners available to record surface data. These scanners employ both mechanical and optical schemes to sample surfaces. The mechanical schemes re-

FIGURE 1.25   Full body scanner. (Photo courtesy of Cyberware.)

quire the operator to trace the surface of the object being scanned with a contact probe. The positional data from the contact probe is recorded. Optical schemes use complex assemblies of cameras and light sources at different angles. Although the final product of the optical scanners is very impressive, some come with a very large price tag. Note that the data collected by these scanners is not fully three-dimensional. It isn't possible to scan the inside of the woman in Figure 1.25, for example. You can only scan the surface of an object, and for each point of the object determine its height. You can think of these scanners as collecting a height field, an image where the pixel values denote the height above some reference level.

VOLUME RENDERING PIPELINE

To make any kind of sense of a group of voxels, you need to be able to view their relationship. This is accomplished via volume rendering.

Volume rendering is achieved by a sequence of operations in a "pipeline." As each operation is completed, the data is passed to the next operation (see Figure 1.26).

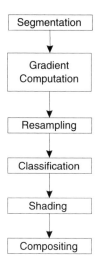

FIGURE 1.26   Volume rendering operations.

The operations in the pipeline consist of segmentation, gradient computation, resampling, classification, shading, and compositing. The order and inclusion of these steps vary among volume rendering implementations. You will soon see that classification can come before or after resampling.

We talked earlier about how three-dimensional data sets are acquired. Most of the methods sample some characteristic that cannot be visualized: density, acoustic impedance, tissue magnetization, and the like. To display this data for visual interpretation sometimes requires assigning color or luminance and opacity to these nonvisual values. This is done by the segmentation and classification stages.

Segmentation is a preprocessing step and typically done before the actual rendering. It is the process of separating the data set into structural units, and something that needs to be done only once to a data set. Segmentation labels voxels in a data set. The label can be any information you want to store with that voxel. You, for example, can label all the voxels of an MRI scan of the human body that belong to tissue, or to bone. After features are identified and segmented, the labels are typically stored together with the voxels on disc.

The labels then can be used in the classification stage in the volume rendering pipeline to assign opacity values and colors to the voxels. You can think of classification as separating voxels into different feature classes, typically done by assigning different opacities and colors to voxels. For example, you could set up the classification stage so that the voxels with the label "bone" get colored gray during rendering, and the voxels with the label "tissue" are assigned green, while making the "tissue" voxels almost completely transparent by assigning a very low opacity value to them.

The combination of segmentation and classification is an extremely powerful feature of the volume rendering pipeline. Segmentation is a very difficult process and hard to capture into an algorithm the computer can perform. Therefore, segmentation often requires the intervention of a human. Classification, on the other hand, is a process that can be completely automated, and therefore is an integral part of the volume rendering pipeline.

The gradient computations find edges or boundaries between different materials. The gradient is a measure of how quickly the data in a data set changes. This information is used in the classification stage and the shading stage.

As imaginary rays are passed through the block of voxels, samples are taken along each ray for accumulation. These sample points are seldom aligned with exact voxel locations. Interpolation is used to generate new values for samples that lie between the actual voxels. The process of generating new addresses into the voxel space and generating new values is called resampling or interpolation.

Shading is used to highlight parts of the data set by using an illumination model. Illumination models can range in complexity. What model you decide to use will depend on a number of parameters including CPU power, number of light sources, and need for color.

Since one pixel on our display may represent hundreds of values we have sampled along a ray, we need a way to accumulate these values into one. Accumulation is accomplished via a composition function. There are two basic functions: front-to-back and back-to-front. Which formula you use depends on which direction you traverse the ray.

FILE FORMAT

Unfortunately, there is no standard file format for three-dimensional sampled data. Applications from different companies use different file formats. However, there are some commonalities among all these file formats.

Typically there is a description of the data. This description can be stored at the beginning of the file, in which case it is called the file header, or it can be stored in a separate file altogether.

This description contains such information as the dimensions (in x, y, and z) of the data, and also the number of bits per sample (intensity resolution). The data may be gray scale or color from a number of different color spaces. The data description may also contain the sample rate (i.e., 1.0mm in y, 1.0mm in y, 0.33mm in z).

Sampling data in three different dimensions creates huge data sets. For example, a file containing data of size 512 × 512 × 512 at 1 byte per sample would be 128 megabytes. If the data contains color data that requires 3 bytes per sample, the file would be 384 megabytes. With files that size, your disk would fill up in a hurry. Some file formats employ data compression techniques to reduce these giant storage requirements. If compression is used, a description of the compression scheme would need to be placed in the data description. Such data compression typically uses simple algorithms such as differential encoding or run length encoding. Complex compression schemes can greatly increase data access time.

The data file format that is used by the programs on the CD-ROM that comes with this book is basically a few bytes of header information (in binary form) followed by the data in pixel packed format, one image after another. The volume consists of stacks of images.

The header is variable length and is comprised of the elements listed below.

```
volume_header
{
    int     magic_number
    int     header_length
    int     width
    int     height
```

```
int      images
int      bits_per_voxel
int      index_bits
float    scaleX
float    scaleY
float    scaleZ
float    rotX
float    rotY
float    rotZ
char     *description
}
```

magic_number:	is just a simple way of versioning
header_length:	is the total number of bytes in the header
width:	is the width, in pixels, of an individual image which makes up the volume. The "x-" value.
height:	is the height, in pixels, of an individual image which makes up the volume. The "y-" value.
images:	is the number of images in the volume. The "z-" value.
bits_per_voxel:	indicates the total number of bits in each voxel, including intensity value and index value
index_bits:	indicates the number of index bits in each voxel
scaleX:	scale value to apply initially to volume in X-direction
scaleY:	scale value to apply initially to volume in Y-direction
scaleZ:	scale value to apply initially to volume in Z-direction
rotateX:	rotation angle about X-axis to apply initially to volume
rotateY:	rotation angle about Y-axis to apply initially to volume

rotateZ: rotation angle about Z-axis to apply initially to volume

description: is an ASCII string describing the data set

The software examples on the CD-ROM require that volume data be formatted according to the specification provided above. A conversion routine is provided with the sample code so you can make modifications to suit the way your data is organized.

The conversion program will handle volumes comprised of multiple images in individual files or multiple images in one file concatenated together. Try using the conversion program on some of your data. It should be fairly straightforward.

The conversion program, **convert,** actually creates two separate files when it is done. The binary volume file (header information and data) are put into a file with a .VOL extension. The program creates another file with a .HDR extension. This file is simply an ASCII version of the header in the .VOL file and is provided for convenience.

FOR FURTHER STUDY

One of the first volume rendering books ever published is [112]. The book is a collection of journal articles that describe the operations of each block in the volume rendering pipeline. Professor Kaufman is one of the world's leading experts in volume rendering and has done a great job of compiling the necessary papers to get someone up and running quickly. Unfortunately at the time of writing (fall 1997) this book is out of print.

For a good text that treats the subject of three-dimensional sampling for medical imaging, see [224]. The construction of two-dimensional images from projections is covered in Section 7.3 of [51] and in [92]. A great introduction to magnetic resonance imaging is [20].

For a technical treatment of confocal microscopy, see [179].

A good paper on the volume rendering pipeline is [129]. Also [43], [206], and [240] go into the volume rendering pipeline in quite some depth.

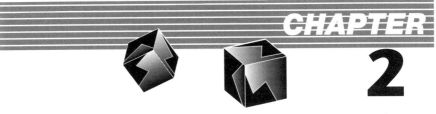

VOLUME RENDERING FRAMEWORK

In order to make effective use of three-dimensional graphics, a certain amount of mathematical modeling is required for spatial management of data. In this chapter we will introduce almost the whole volume rendering pipeline. However the focus is on the mathematics behind orthographic and perspective transformations of a volume data set in order to view it from any angle and distance. All other operations in the volume rendering pipeline will be discussed in detail in subsequent chapters.

OpenGL is an industry standard Application Programming Interface or API for computer graphics. OpenGL defines two-dimensional and three-dimensional graphics pipelines and the way graphics objects are processed and rendered through these pipelines. In the OpenGL API the viewing of an object is controlled using the model, view, and projection matrices. This chapter explains the mathematics behind these matrices, and how they apply to rendering a volume data set.

SPATIAL TRANSFORMS AND LINEAR ALGEBRA

This section will provide some of the mathematical fundamentals needed to understand how to build a volume renderer. We encourage interested readers to seek other references for a thorough introduction to linear algebra.

Graphics primitives can be represented in a Cartesian coordinate space by points with x, y, and z locations. Lines can be represented with two points, polygons with multiple points, and so forth. We can also represent volume sample points by assigning them to x-, y-, and z-locations. The Cartesian space where graphics primitives are defined is considered "object" or model space.

It is very useful to transform graphics primitives in order to realize various views. In order to scale, rotate, and translate primitives, a mathematical relationship for the graphics primitive needs to be defined. A graphics primitive's x-, y-, and z-locations can be transformed to other x'-, y'-, and z'-locations through the use of a mathematical formula. For example, a point can be transformed by the following system of equations where a–o are coefficients describing the relationship of x', y', and z' with respect to x, y, and z.

$$x' = ax + ey + iz + m$$
$$y' = bx + fy + jz + n$$
$$z' = cx + gy + kz + o$$

EQUATION 2.1 A System of linear equations.

Linear algebra allows us to represent a system of equations using matrices. We will see that employing matrices makes representations simpler and allows for descriptions of complex spatial relationships.

The Transformation Matrix

A transformation relationship for a three-dimensional graphics primitive can be described by a 4x4 matrix as follows:

$$\begin{bmatrix} a & e & i & m \\ b & f & j & n \\ c & g & k & o \\ d & h & l & p \end{bmatrix}$$

EQUATION 2.2 A transformation matrix.

Each element and/or group of elements of the transformation matrix perform(s) a specific transformation operation as we will see. The elements d, h, l, and p are required for perspective view representations and homogeneous coordinate resolutions and will be discussed later. For now, we will dismiss this row and consider a simpler 4 × 3 matrix.

Three-dimensional graphics primitives including volume rendered data can be rendered in a parallel projection or a perspective projection. It can be mathematically and computationally more difficult to render a perspective projection. However, since the laws of optics and our life experiences render the three-dimensional world around us in perspective, it is only natural that we desire our computer graphics to follow suit. Perspective projection also provides our brain with valuable cues to help interpret what we see, specifically depth information. Figure 2.1 depicts volume rendered data in parallel and perspective projections. Perspective projection will be discussed in greater detail in a later section.

Transforming a Spatial Location

If a point x, y, and z is represented by a 4 × 1 matrix, it can be multiplied by a 3 × 4 transformation matrix and the result is a 3 × 1 matrix as shown in Equation 2.3.

$$\begin{bmatrix} x' \\ y' \\ z' \end{bmatrix} = \begin{bmatrix} a & e & i & m \\ b & f & j & n \\ c & g & k & o \end{bmatrix} \times \begin{bmatrix} x \\ y \\ z \\ 1 \end{bmatrix}$$

EQUATION 2.3   Matrix multiplication.

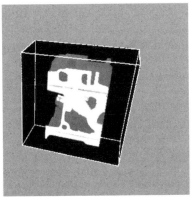

a   b

FIGURE 2.1   Parallel (a) and perspective (b) volume renderings.

Matrix multiplication of these matrices results in the transformation relationship we determined in the beginning represented in Equation (2.1).

MATRIX REPRESENTATIONS AND TRANSFORMATION OPERATIONS

Various spatial relationships can be encoded into a transformation matrix. We will describe some common transformations and what form the matrix takes for each transformation. The following transformations are considered affine transformations since parallel lines within the data set stay parallel after the transformation.

An *identity* transformation results in the original x-, y-, and z-point and appears as shown in Figure 2.2.

An x-, y-, and z-point can be scaled in space using a scale matrix as in Figure 2.3 where sx, sy, and sz are the scale factors that affect the x-, y-, and z-point. Sometimes volumes may not have been sampled or acquired uniformly in the x-, y-, and z-directions. These

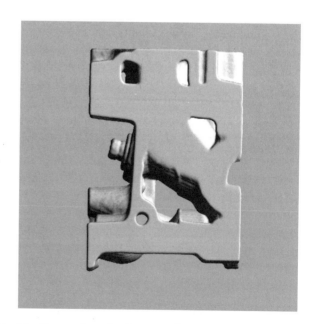

$$\begin{bmatrix} 1 & 0 & 0 & 0 \\ 0 & 1 & 0 & 0 \\ 0 & 0 & 1 & 0 \\ 0 & 0 & 0 & 1 \end{bmatrix}$$

FIGURE 2.2   Identity matrix and volume rendering.

$$\begin{bmatrix} sx & 0 & 0 & 0 \\ 0 & sy & 0 & 0 \\ 0 & 0 & sz & 0 \\ 0 & 0 & 0 & 1 \end{bmatrix}$$

FIGURE 2.3   Scale matrix where $sx = sy = sz = 1.67$ and volume rendering.

volumes are known as anisotropic volumes. An example of an anisotropic volume is an MRI data set where the distance between sample points in the x- and y-directions is 1 mm while the distance between sample points in the z-direction is 1.5 mm. Anisotropic volumes will require either expansion or contraction using a scaling operation. For our example MRI data set, a z-scaling of $1.5x$ is required to balance the rendered volume. Chapter 3 will discuss additional considerations required for volume rendering anisotropic data sets.

Points can also be translated using the matrix in Figure 2.4 where tx, ty, and tz are the values by which the x-, y-, and z-points are translated.

Rotations about the x-, y-, and z-axis can be described by the matrices in Figures 2.5, 2.6, and 2.7.

Note that the rotations described by the matrices are counterclockwise rotations in a right-hand coordinate space. Figure 2.8 shows the relationship of the x-, y-, and z-axis and the direction of rotation about each axis.

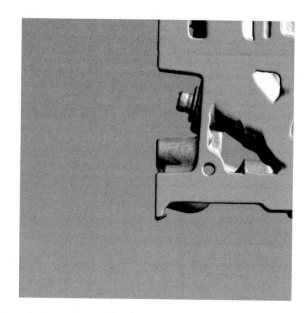

$$\begin{bmatrix} 1 & 0 & 0 & tx \\ 0 & 1 & 0 & ty \\ 0 & 0 & 1 & tz \\ 0 & 0 & 0 & 1 \end{bmatrix}$$

FIGURE 2.4   Translation matrix and volume rendering.

$$\begin{bmatrix} 1 & 0 & 0 & 0 \\ 0 & \cos\Theta & -\sin\Theta & 0 \\ 0 & \sin\Theta & \cos\Theta & 0 \\ 0 & 0 & 0 & 1 \end{bmatrix}$$

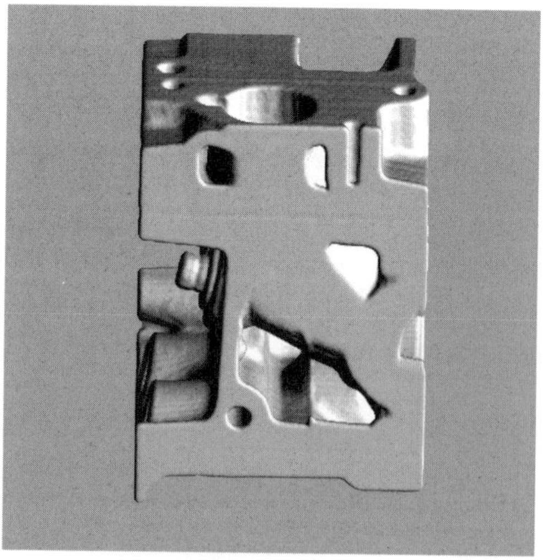

FIGURE 2.5   Rotation about *x*-axis matrix and volume rendering.

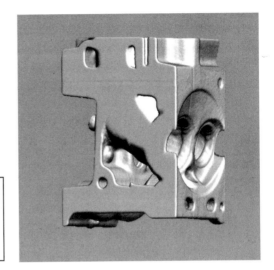

$$\begin{bmatrix} \cos\Theta & 0 & \sin\Theta & 0 \\ 0 & 1 & 0 & 0 \\ -\sin\Theta & 0 & \cos\Theta & 0 \\ 0 & 0 & 0 & 1 \end{bmatrix}$$

FIGURE 2.6 Rotation about *y*-axis matrix and volume rendering.

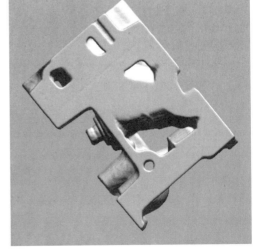

$$\begin{bmatrix} \cos\Theta & -\sin\Theta & 0 & 0 \\ \sin\Theta & \cos\Theta & 0 & 0 \\ 0 & 0 & 1 & 0 \\ 0 & 0 & 0 & 1 \end{bmatrix}$$

FIGURE 2.7 Rotation about *z*-axis matrix and volume rendering.

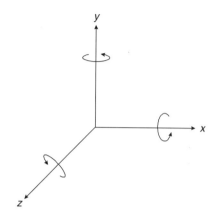

FIGURE 2.8   A right-handed coordinate axis and counterclockwise rotations.

The power of matrix representation becomes apparent when several transformations are combined into a single matrix representation. Any combination of the matrices presented above can be combined to produce compound transformations. Matrices are combined by performing a matrix multiplication. Using linear algebra, the columns and rows of the equivalent 4 × 4 matrices can be multiplied and summed as shown in Figure 2.9.

Note that matrix multiplication is not a commutative operation and different orders of operations can result in differing products. This implies that if $M = M1 \times M2$ and $M' = M2 \times M1$ but that M does not equal M'.

For example, consider two matrices that will be combined. The first is the matrix Rx which is a matrix that specifies some rotation about the x-axis. The second matrix is Tz which is a matrix that specifies some translation in the z-direction. The expression $M = Rx \times Tz$ will result in a matrix that would translate an object in the z-direction and then perform a rotation about the x-axis relative to the x-, y-, and z-coordinates specified by the translation matrix Tz. However, the expression $M' = Tz \times Rx$ will result in a matrix that would rotate an object about the x-axis and then perform a translation in the z-direction relative to the x-, y-, and z-coordinates specified by the rotation matrix Rx. This implies that the co-ordinates will have been rotated about the x-axis. In other words,

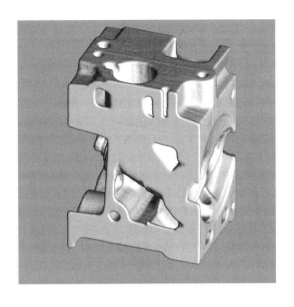

$$\begin{bmatrix} a' & e' & i' & m' \\ b' & f' & j' & n' \\ c' & g' & k' & o' \\ d' & h' & l' & p' \end{bmatrix} = \begin{bmatrix} a1 & e1 & i1 & m1 \\ b1 & f1 & j1 & n1 \\ c1 & g1 & k1 & o1 \\ d1 & h1 & l1 & p1 \end{bmatrix} \times \begin{bmatrix} a2 & e2 & i2 & m2 \\ b2 & f2 & j2 & n2 \\ c2 & g2 & k2 & o2 \\ d2 & h2 & l2 & p2 \end{bmatrix}$$

$a' = (a1 \times a2) + (e1 \times b2) + (i1 \times c2) + (m1 \times d2)$
$b' = (b1 \times a2) + (f1 \times b2) + (j1 \times c2) + (n1 \times d2)$
$c' = (c1 \times a2) + (g1 \times b2) + (k1 \times c2) + (o1 \times d2)$
$d' = (d1 \times a2) + (h1 \times b2) + (l1 \times c2) + (p1 \times d2)$

$e' = (a1 \times e2) + (e1 \times f2) + (i1 \times g2) + (m1 \times h2)$
$f' = (b1 \times e2) + (f1 \times f2) + (j1 \times g2) + (n1 \times h2)$
$g' = (c1 \times e2) + (g1 \times f2) + (k1 \times g2) + (o1 \times h2)$
$h' = (d1 \times e2) + (h1 \times f2) + (l1 \times g2) + (p1 \times h2)$

$i' = (a1 \times i2) + (e1 \times j2) + (i1 \times k2) + (m1 \times l2)$
$j' = (b1 \times i2) + (f1 \times j2) + (j1 \times k2) + (n1 \times l2)$
$k' = (c1 \times i2) + (g1 \times j2) + (k1 \times k2) + (o1 \times l2)$
$l' = (d1 \times i2) + (h1 \times j2) + (l1 \times k2) + (p1 \times l2)$

$m' = (a1 \times m2) + (e1 \times n2) + (i1 \times o2) + (m1 \times p2)$
$n' = (b1 \times m2) + (f1 \times n2) + (j1 \times o2) + (n1 \times p2)$
$o' = (c1 \times m2) + (g1 \times n2) + (k1 \times o2) + (o1 \times p2)$
$p' = (d1 \times m2) + (h1 \times n2) + (l1 \times o2) + (p1 \times p2)$

FIGURE 2.9 Compound matrix and volume rendering. In this case a rotation around the x-axis and y-axis.

43

the transformation described in the right-most matrix will be applied first.

We can see that these tools of specifying simple, discrete spatial transformations can be combined to specify quite complex views and spatial relationships.

Volumes typically are addressed from one corner. That is, one corner is assigned the location (0, 0, 0) and all other voxels are addressed relative to this voxel. When scaling or rotating a volume of voxels, the transformation should first specify a translation of the volume such that the center of the volume is at the origin or (0, 0, 0) point before performing a scale or rotation operation. After all scales and rotations have been performed, the volume can be translated back to where the viewable window space is defined. All of these discrete operations can be combined into one matrix and transformation operation. However, from our discussion of the importance of matrix multiplication order, you should take care in specifying the correct combination of discrete transformations.

Linear algebra defines that a matrix is invertible if its determinant is nonzero. For practically all properly defined affine graphical transformations and their combinations, the matrices are invertible. The inverse of a matrix is especially useful since we can now take the x'-, y'-, and z'-points and transform them back to the original x-, y-, and z-points in *object* space. We will take advantage of this capability later when we build our volume renderer.

RASTERIZATION AND RENDERING A VOLUME

Now that we are able to transform a point, we can address the transformation of voxels belonging to a volume. By assigning each voxel the x-, y-, and z-location of its sample relative to the volume as a whole, a three-dimensional transformation matrix can be used to scale, rotate, and translate each voxel in the volume to another location in the same object space.

Each voxel assigned an x-, y-, and z-location can be transformed given a transformation matrix into a new x'-, y'-, and z'-location. To view this volume we need to paint two-dimensional image pixels on a screen with various colors representing the transformed voxels. Figure 2.10 shows a two-dimensional depiction of a transformed volume and how the transformed voxels will be projected onto a one-dimensional plane (or line in this case). The figure is a simplification of the three-dimensional volume rendering problem but is an effective representation. The transformation of voxels and projection onto a two-dimensional plane raises three problems. First, how are we going to resolve the fact that we have multiple z-values represented at most x- and y-points on the image plane? Second, since the transformation process generates real values, voxels are projected onto locations between projection plane pixels. What do we do with the fractional components of x'-, y'-, and z'? Since we would like to paint this volume onto a two-dimensional pixel plane, we need to resolve the fractional voxel locations that need to map onto the two-dimensional discrete space. Third, for some transformations, especially scaling, there is not a very good one-to-one correspondence of voxels to pixels in the two-dimensional display plane and the resulting image can have *holes* where voxel samples are missing. These problems are shown in Figure 2.10.

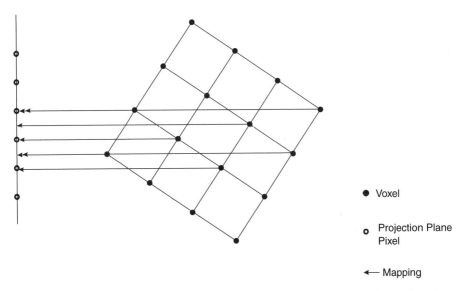

FIGURE 2.10 Transformed volume and mapping to "image" space. Also called forward mapping.

To address the first problem, having multiple z-values, we use compositing. Compositing essentially takes a series of voxels and determines which pixel value will be the result of collapsing the series of voxel values, or values derived from the voxel values, into one pixel color. Compositing details will be discussed in Chapter 6.

The second problem, what to do with the fractional component, can be overcome by applying a filter to the voxel values that weights the contributions of the voxels as they are mapped to two-dimensional pixels.

The third problem is similar to the second in that a method is needed to take the transformed voxel and determine how it will be painted onto portions of several pixels to eliminate *holes*. One solution to the *hole* problem is known as splatting which applies a filtering operation to voxel values and can be used to overcome the second problem as well. Splatting takes an x' and y' real location and "splats" that color onto a location of two-dimensional discrete pixels. Figure 2.11 shows an example of splatting.

A method for transforming a volume of voxels and the problem of two-dimensional representation has been discussed. We could go into greater detail of how this can be implemented and discuss

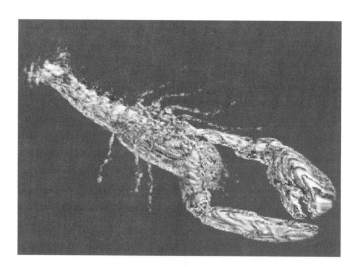

FIGURE 2.11   Employing the splatting technique. (Data set courtesy of Bob Mazaika of Advanced Visual Systems, and Mark Kessler, University of Michigan Medical School.)

the limitations of the solution. However, let us examine an alternative way of approaching the volume transformation and representation problem that is straightforward and offers a great many more advantages for implementation.

Forward Versus Inverse Transformation: A Matter of Relativity

Instead of transforming the individual voxel values and then determining the mapping onto a two-dimensional plane, we will examine the problem from the perspective of the two-dimensional plane where the final image will be viewed. Since the process of transforming from the original volume to the two-dimensional projection plane can be described by a transformation matrix **M,** then the process of transforming from the two-dimensional projection plane back to the original volume can be described by the inverse of the transformation matrix **M.** We also call this *forward* and *inverse mapping,* respectively. As we will see, the concept of inverse mapping can be used to our advantage in performing volume rendering. Figure 2.12 shows that by aligning with the two-dimensional projection plane, we can cast, or map, rays through voxel space, and the problem is now simplified.

Casting Rays in Inverse Mapping

By looking at the world relative to the projection plane, we make life easier for ourselves. Address a discrete x'- and y'-location in the projection plane and for that location imagine an infinite series of discrete z'-values going through voxel space. In practice, it can be shown that a determinant range of discrete z'-values can be found for each x'- and y'-image space location. The *inverse transformation* allows us to take the discrete x'-, y'-, and z'-values and transform them back to the real location values $x, y,$ and z in the original voxel space. This method is what we, and many others, call *ray casting.*

The arrows shown in Figure 2.12 depict rays that are cast through the transformed volume. The x's depicted in Figure 2.12 are the sample points where the volume voxels will contribute to the sampled value. This operation where we need to determine the

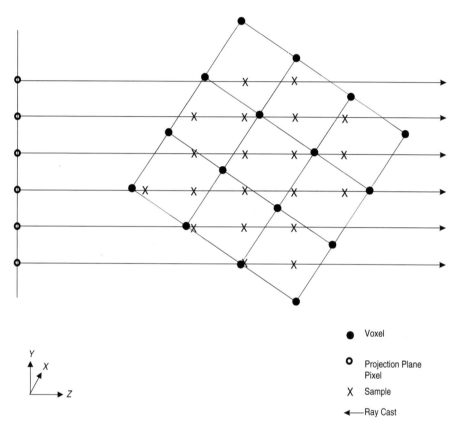

FIGURE 2.12 Transformed "image" space and mapping onto a volume. Also called inverse mapping.

value of a sample within a neighborhood of discrete grid values is known as resampling and is discussed in detail in Chapter 5. Using ray casting, we have eliminated the problem of holes since we will have volume voxels that contribute to every interesting two-dimensional pixel value in the projection plane. Scaling transformations will no longer have the potential of producing holes in the final image. However, we still need to resolve the compositing problem where multiple sample points must be condensed into a single projection plane pixel and the resampling problem that arose from results of the real transformation.

To solve the resampling problem, we need to use interpolation which results in a single value that is representative of the neighborhood of values surrounding the sample. Let us for now simply round the real x-, y-, and z-values by adding 0.5 to each x-, y-, and z-value and truncating the values to integers. This approach is known as nearest neighbor interpolation and is one of the simplest forms of interpolation. Chapter 5 discusses more advanced schemes for interpolation among a neighborhood of voxels.

Accumulation and Compositing along a Ray

Now that we are able to transform a series of rays, we will discuss the problem of resolving multiple z'-sample values for a ray. For each discrete sample along a ray located at x' and y', a voxel value is determined by interpolating among a neighborhood of voxels located about the real position x, y, and z within the volume. Since the viewable image on the projection plane can bear only a single value, we have two choices. We can choose only one sample along the ray and assign that to the pixel on the projection plane, or we need to formulate a derived value using all the samples on one ray.

We call this operation of formulating the pixel value *compositing*. A very simple compositing operation is accomplished by choosing the greatest scalar value along the ray. This is the first choice we outlined above. This compositing scheme is known as *maximum intensity projection*. Though it is very simple and intuitive, it is very effective for viewing isolated structures with very little surrounding noise such as arteries and veins in medical angiographic data sets. Figure 2.13 shows a volume rendering using the maximum intensity projection compositing rule (note the blood vessels that are brightly depicted in the rendering). In Chapter 6 we will discuss more advanced compositing operations.

Color (RGB)

A rendered volume to this point has always consisted of a single scalar value that varies in intensity and can be represented by a gray scale of shades. But how do we get color into our images? We can assign a color value to each voxel in the data set we are rendering.

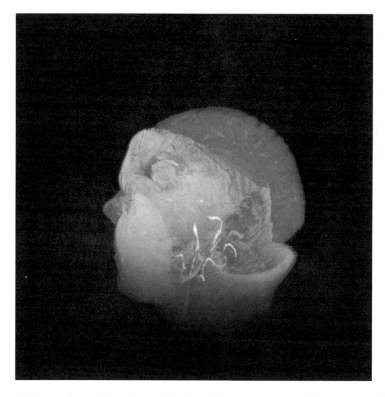

FIGURE 2.13 Maximum intensity projection. The major veins and arteries are clearly visible.

A color can be assigned to a particular scalar voxel value through the use of a color look-up table. The look-up table typically uses the voxel scalar value as input and assigns colors in the appropriate color model. Red, green, and blue color assignments are common for many volume rendering implementations since many display and graphics hardware systems support RGB representation, but any color model can be used if you so desire.

How to assign color values to voxels will be discussed in greater depth when segmentation and shading are introduced in Chapter 4. Color voxels offer complexities to the compositing problem. These and many more issues will be addressed later in Chapter 6.

Transparency and Opacity (Alpha)

In addition to color, voxels can also assume a degree of transparency or opacity. A normalized value from 0.0 to 1.0, called alpha, is used to represent the degree of opacity. An alpha value is assigned to a voxel through the use of classification. For example, an opacity value of 0.0 means that the voxel is completely transparent and an opacity value of 1.0 means that the voxel is completely opaque. If the opacity of a voxel along a ray is not 1.0 or fully opaque, the opacity must be incorporated into the compositing equation. Opacity will be discussed when compositing is explained in Chapter 6. By strategically assigning opacity or alpha values, parts of the volume can appear transparent. This allows you to remove or "see through" the features of little interest so you can focus on the structure or data of particular interest.

COMPOSITING OF MULTIPLE VOLUMES AND OTHER PRIMITIVES

Rendering a single volume is a very challenging and compute-intensive operation in itself. However, for practical applications there is a need to combine multiple volumes and sometimes even geometric primitives into the volume for enhancing the volume visualization result.

When multiple, intersecting volumes are rendered in a single scene, we need to give special consideration to coalescing the samples from each volume along a ray. We need to apply compositing logic or mathematical expressions to all co-located samples along the ray before all the z-samples can be composited for the ray.

When combining a volume data set with computer graphics primitives such as solid lines and polygons, the combination can be accomplished after the geometry is rendered by employing a z-buffer test as the volume is rendered. If the test indicates that a volume is located behind some opaque geometry, then the volume sample will not contribute to the composition along the ray. If the volume sample is in front of the opaque geometry, then the color of the geometry will be incorporated into the ray composition.

The problem of combining a volume with translucent geometry requires an approach similar to combining multiple volumes. The

z-buffer is not sufficient since we actually need a color and opacity sample as well as a z-value from each of the translucent geometric primitives to blend with the sample from the volume. Again, some rules for mixing co-located samples need to be applied before the representative sample along the ray can be blended.

PERSPECTIVE AND ORTHOGRAPHIC PROJECTIONS

We have briefly introduced almost all of the operations in the volume rendering pipeline: resampling, classification, assigning colors to voxel values, and compositing. So far we have not discussed gradient computation and shading, which are the topics of the next chapter. We will now delve into the theory and mathematics behind orthographic and perspective renderings of a volume data set, as we showed in Figure 2.1.

All object transformations discussed to this point have been viewed using an orthographic or parallel projection. Parallel projections are characterized by casting parallel rays which extend to infinity. The simplest form of parallel projection is the identity transformation, shown in Figure 2.2. Projections are combined with transformations which we discussed earlier and affect the model or object and the view. Since the parallel projection can be represented by the identity matrix, the combination of parallel projection and object transformations results in only the object transformations.

A perspective projection is characterized by the foreshortening of objects in a scene, where objects far away appear smaller than objects that are closer to the viewer. In order to generate a perspective image, we cast rays in the shape of a frustum, which is a pyramid with the tip cut off as shown in Figures 2.14 and 2.15. The perspective image we want to render is projected onto the smaller rectangle closer to the apex of the pyramid, as indicated with the line labeled "near" in Figure 2.15. The perspective projection operation can be represented with a special projection matrix shown in Equation (2.3).

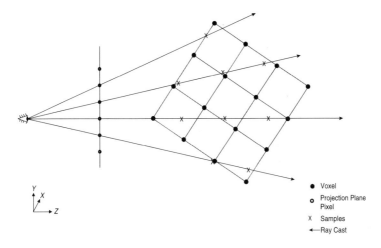

FIGURE 2.14 The perspective ray casting.

$$\begin{bmatrix} \dfrac{2 \times near}{right - left} & 0 & A & 0 \\ 0 & \dfrac{2 \times near}{top - bottom} & B & 0 \\ 0 & 0 & C & D \\ 0 & 0 & -1 & 0 \end{bmatrix}$$

$$A = \frac{right + left}{right - left}$$

$$B = \frac{top + bottom}{top - bottom}$$

$$C = -\frac{far + near}{far - near}$$

$$D = -\frac{2 \times far \times near}{far - near}$$

EQUATION 2.3 Perspective projection matrix representation.

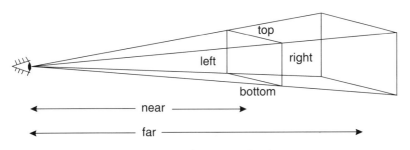

FIGURE 2.15 The perspective frustum.

Just as in OpenGL we separate the transformation of the volume from the actual projection onto the screen. OpenGL uses two matrices to describe the transformation of an object: the model matrix **M** and the view matrix **V**. It is also quite common to combine these two matrices into one matrix, the Model-View matrix, or **MV**. That is what we have assumed in this book. We have referred and will refer to this matrix as the transformation matrix. Separating the transformation and projection into two matrices has the advantage that the positioning of the volume in three-dimensional space is separate from the actual rendering, orthographic or perspective.

As we have stated before, the identity matrix is the simplest form of the orthographic projection matrix. The general form of a orthographic projection matrix is given in Equation (2.4). This matrix represents a scaling in x, y, and z as well as a translation. A characteristic of an orthographic matrix is that the bottom row is always 0,0,0,1.

$$\begin{bmatrix} \dfrac{2}{right - left} & 0 & 0 & t_x \\ 0 & \dfrac{2}{top - bottom} & 0 & t_y \\ 0 & 0 & \dfrac{-2}{far - near} & t_z \\ 0 & 0 & 0 & 1 \end{bmatrix}$$

where

$$t_x = \frac{right + left}{right - left}$$

$$t_y = \frac{top + bottom}{top - bottom}$$

$$t_z = -\frac{far + near}{far - near}$$

EQUATION 2.4   Orthographic projection matrix representation.

Instead of casting rays through the volume in the shape of a frustum, we cast rays in the shape of a box through the volume for orthographic projections. This is shown in Figure 2.16. As you can see there is no scaling of an object that lies within the box.

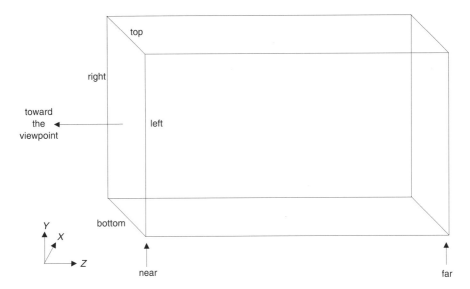

FIGURE 2.16   Orthographic projection cube.

The Forward Perspective Projection and Transformation

The perspective projection matrix in Equation 2.3 has added some complexity to our object transformation operation. Matrix parameters d, h, l and p in Equation (2.2) are not simply 0, 0, 0, and 1 when matrices are combined as they were when only orthographic transformations are allowed.

To get a better feel for the use of perspective projection along with an object or model and view transformation, we will follow a point or vertex through each of these transformations.

We start with a point in object space whose coordinates are

$$\begin{bmatrix} x \\ y \\ z \\ w \end{bmatrix} \text{ where } w = 1$$

Here we represented the point in a homogeneous coordinate system. This means that we add an extra parameter, the homogeneous coordinate "w" to the vector. One of the reasons to do this is to allow scaling, rotation, and translation to all be represented in one 4 × 4 matrix and treated as matrix multiplications. If we do not add "w" we can have only a 3 × 3 transformation matrix, and it then is no longer possible to represent translations in that 3 × 3 matrix. As long as we keep $w = 1$, the homogeneous point $[x,y,z,1]$ corresponds to the three-dimensional point $[x,y,z]$. Refer to the For Further Study section for more information on this topic.

Next we combine both the model-view transformation matrix and the projection matrix into one, as we show in Equation (2.5).

$$\begin{bmatrix} aM & eM & iM & mM \\ bM & fM & jM & nM \\ cM & gM & kM & oM \\ 0 & 0 & 0 & 1 \end{bmatrix} \times \begin{bmatrix} aP & 0 & iP & 0 \\ 0 & fP & jP & 0 \\ 0 & 0 & kP & oP \\ 0 & 0 & -1 & 0 \end{bmatrix}$$

$$= \begin{bmatrix} a & e & i & m \\ b & f & j & n \\ c & g & k & o \\ d & h & l & p \end{bmatrix}$$

EQUATION 2.5   Combined perspective model-view matrix.

The model-view matrix is the left-most matrix, multiplied with the perspective matrix results in the combined matrix.

Now we multiply a point, $[x, y, z, 1]$, by this combined matrix to transform it into clip coordinate space.

$$\begin{bmatrix} a & e & i & m \\ b & f & j & n \\ c & g & k & o \\ d & h & l & p \end{bmatrix} \times \begin{bmatrix} x \\ y \\ z \\ 1 \end{bmatrix} = \begin{bmatrix} x' \\ y' \\ z' \\ w' \end{bmatrix}$$

$x' = (a * x) + (e * y) + (i * z) + m$
$y' = (b * x) + (f * y) + (j * z) + n$
$z' = (c * x) + (g * y) + (k * z) + o$
$w' = (d * x) + (h * y) + (l * z) + p$

Next we need to divide the resulting x', y', and z' by the homogeneous coordinate w' to keep the homogeneous coordinate w

equal to 1. This operation is called the perspective divide, which transforms the point into normalized device coordinates.

$$x'' = \frac{x'}{w'}$$

$$y'' = \frac{y'}{w'}$$

$$z'' = \frac{z'}{w'}$$

$$w'' = \frac{w'}{w'} = 1$$

Since window coordinates are typically positive integers, the transformed and projected coordinates in normalized device space must be subjected to yet another transformation. In the OpenGL model this is called a viewport transformation which is simply a scaling and translation in the two-dimensional projection image space. Thus the x''- and y''-coordinates can be scaled and offset resulting in i and j for final rendering using a two-dimensional viewport transformation.

$$i = (Sx * x'') + Tx$$
$$j = (Sy * y'') + Ty$$

Now we have the final pixel coordinate (i,j) in image or window space.

The Forward Orthographic Transformation and Projection

The orthographic case is a special case of the perspective one. Instead of using the perspective projection matrix in Equation (2.5) we use the orthographic projection matrix. This in turn means that we do not need to do a perspective divide anymore, since the homogeneous coordinate "w" will always equal 1. We leave it to the reader to verify.

The Inverse Perspective Transformation and Projection

You might conclude that the forward transformation and projection is all very good for geometric transformations, but what about volume rendering? Earlier, we discussed how the inverse transformation is a very favorable method when performing ray casting. One solution can be found by evaluating the inverse of the procedure just presented.

The combined perspective matrix in Equation (2.5) has the characteristic of being invertible. This is very convenient for us. By inverting the combined model-view and projection matrix and by reversing the viewport transformation, we are able to move from destination image projection space back to the model or object space where the volume data set is easily addressable. This is shown below.

We start by reversing the viewport transformation and scaling and biasing i and j into x'', and y''. The z''-coordinate will assume the range of values that are being "cast" by the ray. We will set the homogenous coordinate w'' to the value of 1. See also Figure 2.14.

$$x'' = \frac{(i - Tx)}{Sx}$$

$$y'' = \frac{(j - Ty)}{Sy}$$

z'' (ranges from some starting value to an ending value on the ray being cast)

$w'' = 1$

Next, we transform this point using the inverse of the combined model-view and perspective transformation matrices.

$$\begin{bmatrix} al & el & il & ml \\ bl & fl & jl & nl \\ cl & gl & kl & ol \\ dl & hl & ll & pl \end{bmatrix} = inverse\left(\begin{bmatrix} a & e & i & m \\ b & f & j & n \\ c & g & k & o \\ d & h & l & p \end{bmatrix}\right)$$

$$\begin{bmatrix} al & el & il & ml \\ bl & fl & jl & nl \\ cl & gl & kl & ol \\ dl & hl & ll & pl \end{bmatrix} \times \begin{bmatrix} x'' \\ y'' \\ z'' \\ 1 \end{bmatrix} = \begin{bmatrix} x' \\ y' \\ z' \\ w' \end{bmatrix}$$

Finally, we perform the perspective divide operation.

$$x = \frac{x'}{w'}$$

$$y = \frac{y'}{w'}$$

$$z = \frac{z'}{w'}$$

$$w = \frac{w'}{w'} = 1$$

We now have the homogeneous point $[x,y,z,1]$, which is the same as the point $[x,y,z]$ in three-dimensional voxel or object space. If this point falls inside the data set we are rendering, we can now perform resampling, assign colors and opacities, and composite a result, as discussed earlier. Once this is done we increase z'' by some value, usually 1, and do the whole process again, until the resulting point $[x,y,z]$ does not fall inside the data set anymore. Then we move on to the next pixel $(i + 1, j)$ until we have processed the whole image.

The Inverse Orthographic Transformation and Projection

As you probably suspect this is also a special case of the perspective transformation. We cast a ray from image space through the transformed volume. For each sample point on the ray we need to find the $[x,y,z]$ point in object or voxel space.

We again start by reversing the viewport transformation and scaling and biasing i and j into x'', and y''. The z'' coordinate will assume the range of values that are being "cast" by the ray. We will set the homogenous coordinate w'' to the value of 1.

$$x'' = \frac{(i - Tx)}{Sx}$$

$$y'' = \frac{(j - Ty)}{Sy}$$

z'' (ranges from some starting value to an ending value on the ray being cast)

$w'' = 1$

Next, we transform this point using the inverse of the combined model-view and orthographic transformation matrices.

$$\begin{bmatrix} al & el & il & ml \\ bl & fl & jl & nl \\ cl & gl & kl & ol \\ 0 & 0 & 0 & 1 \end{bmatrix} = inverse \left(\begin{bmatrix} a & e & i & m \\ b & f & j & n \\ c & g & k & o \\ 0 & 0 & 0 & 1 \end{bmatrix} \right)$$

$$\begin{bmatrix} al & el & il & ml \\ bl & fl & jl & nl \\ cl & gl & kl & ol \\ 0 & 0 & 0 & 1 \end{bmatrix} \times \begin{bmatrix} x'' \\ y'' \\ z'' \\ 1 \end{bmatrix} = \begin{bmatrix} x' \\ y' \\ z' \\ 1 \end{bmatrix}$$

We now have the homogeneous point $[x',y',z',1]$, which is the same as the point $[x,y,z]$ in three-dimensional voxel or object space. If this point falls inside the data set we are rendering, we can now perform the resampling, assigning colors and opacities and compositing operations, as discussed earlier. Once this is done we increase z'' by some value, usually 1, and do the whole process again, until the resulting point $[x,y,z]$ does not fall inside the data set anymore. Then we move on to the next pixel $(i + 1, j)$ until we have processed the whole image.

Computing $[x',y',z',1]$ for every sample point on a ray takes a lot of processing power. Fortunately there is an easy optimization step we can perform. For each sample point on a ray we only increase z'' with some value dz'' and leave x'' and y'' constant. If we set $dz''=1$ we get

$$\begin{bmatrix} al & el & il & ml \\ bl & fl & jl & nl \\ cl & gl & kl & ol \\ 0 & 0 & 0 & 1 \end{bmatrix} \times \begin{bmatrix} x'' \\ y'' \\ z'' + dz'' \\ 1 \end{bmatrix} = \begin{bmatrix} x' + il \\ y' + jl \\ z' + kl \\ 1 \end{bmatrix}$$

As you can see we only need to add the third column vector $[il,jl,kl,0]$ of the combined matrix to the result of the previous computation, $[x',y',z',1]$, to get the new point. Thus instead of doing a full matrix multiplication for each sample point, we only need to calculate that once at the beginning of each ray, and for all other sample points along the ray we can just add a constant increment. This saves a lot of compute power.

Something similar can be done for the perspective case, but it is somewhat more complicated. How this is done is explained in the next section.

The Perspective Ray Transform

Even though the inverse perspective transformation is an elegant solution, it is very expensive in terms of computation. Each sample point is subjected to a (16 multiplies) and (12 additions) operation in addition to (4 divides). Even with some z-stepping optimizations, this still requires (4 additions) and (4 divides) for each subsequent sample point.

The ray casting method lends itself to a much more computationally efficient solution. By isolating each ray that is cast such that traversal on that ray is described by a transformation, it is possible to reduce the problem to a simple orthographic transformation relative to the ray being cast. If we refer back to Figure 2.15, we can see that the frustum is simply a reflection of this ray-casting model.

By addressing a single ray independently, the slope of the ray at a point x and y with respect to a parallel ray at the origin is depicted as a 2D projection in Figure 2.17. The relationship is described by the following equations where d is the projection plane referred to as the *near* plane in the original perspective matrix, Equation (2.3).

$$iR = x''/d$$
$$jR = y''/d$$

Each ray has its own transformation matrix and that transformation matrix is an orthographic matrix as shown in Equation (2.6). As a result, for each ray a unique "ray transform" can be described and combined with the inverse of the model-view matrix to produce a fast, orthographic ray stepping prescription for volume rendering. The "ray transform" reduces the computation z-step optimization to only (3 additions) for each subsequent sample, which is the same for an orthographic projection. There is, however, an optimized setup cost of (4 multiples) and (4 additions) per ray cast.

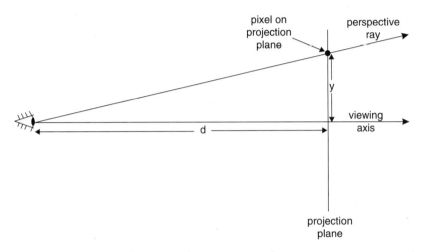

FIGURE 2.17   The ray transform: Transforming a view direction ray into a perspective ray.

$$
\begin{bmatrix}
1 & 0 & iR & 0 \\
0 & 1 & jR & 0 \\
0 & 0 & 1 & 0 \\
0 & 0 & 0 & 1
\end{bmatrix}
$$

EQUATION 2.6   The ray transform.

To demonstrate, let's start with an image space coordinate

$$
\begin{bmatrix}
x'' \\
y'' \\
z'' \\
1
\end{bmatrix}
$$

and a model-view (orthographic matrix) and a ray transform for this particular "x" and "y" ray. The inverse of the model-view matrix and the ray transform can be combined into one matrix. We start with the model-view matrix

$$\begin{bmatrix} aM & eM & iM & mM \\ bM & fM & jM & nM \\ cM & gM & kM & oM \\ 0 & 0 & 0 & 1 \end{bmatrix}$$

Then compute the inverse of the model-view matrix and multiply by the ray transform results in

$$inverse\left(\begin{bmatrix} aM & eM & iM & mM \\ bM & fM & jM & nM \\ cM & gM & kM & oM \\ 0 & 0 & 0 & 1 \end{bmatrix}\right) \times \begin{bmatrix} 1 & 0 & iR & 0 \\ 0 & 1 & jR & 0 \\ 0 & 0 & 1 & 0 \\ 0 & 0 & 0 & 1 \end{bmatrix}$$

$$= \begin{bmatrix} a & e & i & m \\ b & f & j & n \\ c & g & k & o \\ 0 & 0 & 0 & 1 \end{bmatrix}$$

which is the combined inverse of the model-view matrix and ray transform.

Next transform the sample point from destination space to source space:

$$\begin{bmatrix} a & e & i & m \\ b & f & j & n \\ c & g & k & o \\ 0 & 0 & 0 & 1 \end{bmatrix} \times \begin{bmatrix} x'' \\ y'' \\ z'' \\ 1 \end{bmatrix} = \begin{bmatrix} x' \\ y' \\ z' \\ 1 \end{bmatrix}$$

$x' = (a * x) + (e * y) + (i * z) + m$
$y' = (b * x) + (f * y) + (j * z) + n$
$z' = (c * x) + (g * y) + (k * z) + o$

We now have the homogeneous point $[x',y',z',1]$, which is the same as the point $[x, y, z]$ in three-dimensional voxel or object space. If this point falls within the data set, we can now perform the resampling and assign colors and opacities and composite results, as discussed earlier. Once this is done we increment z'' by some value, usually 1, and do the whole process again, until the resulting point [x, y, z] does not fall within the data set anymore. We then move on to the next pixel (i + 1, j) until we have processed the whole image.

FOR FURTHER STUDY

More information on transformations, homogeneous versus nonhomogeneous coordinate systems, projections, and more can be found in [65]. The OpenGL programming guide [18] is a good book for in depth explanation of the OpenGL viewing model. The OpenGL reference guide [19] is another good resource to have.

In [10] there is more on transformations, maximum intensity projection, and compositing in general. In [272] you will find examples of volume renderings done in YUV color space.

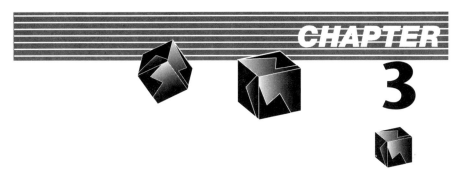

ILLUMINATION AND SHADING

Illumination and shading refer to well-known techniques in conventional computer graphics to greatly enhance the appearance of a geometric model that is being rendered. Shading tries to model effects like shadows, light scattering, and absorption that occur in the real world when light falls on an object. In conventional computer graphics the goal is to render an image with near photographic quality, which resembles the real world. See Figure 1.1(a) in Chapter 1 for an example of a photo-realistic rendered geometric scene.

In our discussion we adopt the same terminology as in the computer graphics standard work [65]. An illumination model describes the way a color is assigned to a point in space, based on the light that shines on it, the angle between viewer and light, the material properties, and the orientation and position in space. A shading model is the framework in which an illumination model fits. The shading model determines when the illumination model is applied to a point, what parameters the illumination model gets, or even which illumination model is to be used. This distinction between shading and illumination is important later when we discuss shading and illumination models.

In volume rendering, photo realism is not the primary goal. Instead the primary goal of shading is to enhance the visual understanding of the data set one is looking at. The goal is to get better spatial cues and structural information about the data set. Sometimes it is better to do no shading at all! A volume data set is a representation of an object and its internals. This data set can represent a part of a human body, an engine block, or layers in the earth's crust. When you look at these in the real world, you cannot even see the inside of these objects. Therefore it is not as important to shade the inside as realistically as possible, since there may not be an immediate reference to what it would look like in the real world in the first place.

This chapter will first discuss gradient calculation. The gradient can be thought of as a surface normal. The gradient is used in the lighting and classification stages of the volume rendering pipeline. Classification is the topic of the next chapter. Two commonly used shading models, Phong and Gouraud shading, are discussed. Examples are given that demonstrate the use of shading and what it means to the final rendered image.

THE GRADIENT

The gradient is a measure of how quickly voxel intensities in a data set change. It also tells you the direction of the change. This is important information in volume rendering because it tells you something about the structure of the data set. Two different metals in an engine, for example, will probably have different voxel intensities in your data set. Therefore the gradient will be significant at the boundary of those two metals. The direction of the gradient also tells you what the orientation of that boundary is. The volume rendering pipeline calculates a gradient for every voxel in the data set.

The gradient is a three-dimensional vector (see Figure 3.1). We use the symbol ∇ for it.

$$\nabla = [x, y, z] \tag{3.1}$$

The gradient has orientation information because it is a vector that points a certain direction in three-dimensional space. Therefore it can tell you something about the orientation of a structure in a data set.

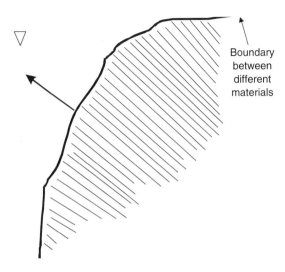

∇

Boundary
between
different
materials

FIGURE 3.1 A boundary between two materials and the gradient vector.

The gradient magnitude also is important. You can think of the magnitude of a vector as its length. The gradient magnitude is

$$|\nabla| = \sqrt{x^2 + y^2 + z^2} \tag{3.2}$$

It tells you something about how quickly data changes in your data set. If the gradient magnitude is zero, it means that there was no change in voxel values in a voxel neighborhood.

We explained earlier what the gradient means intuitively, but what does it mean mathematically? To answer that question we will have to resort to some signal processing (see Figure 3.2). To understand how gradient computation works you will need to understand interpolation first. You will find an in-depth discussion of interpolation in Chapter 5. Here we will give you a brief introduction.

Interpolation computes intermediate values between two discrete points. Interpolation makes sense only if we believe we can reconstruct the underlying continuous function using the discrete voxels in a data set. Figure 3.2(a) shows an example of discrete voxels in one dimension. Figure 3.2(b) shows the underlying continuous function these voxels represent. You can think of interpolation as a two-step process. First we reconstruct the original continuous

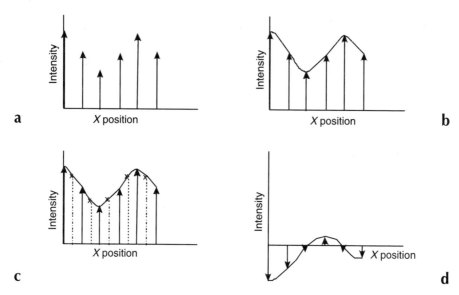

FIGURE 3.2 (a) Discrete data; (b) discrete data and the underlying continuous function; (c) newly interpolated points by sampling the continuous function; (d) the derivative of the continuous function and sampled points.

function from the voxels in the data set [Figure 3.2(b)]. Then we re-sample the reconstructed, continuous function at the places we are interested in to create a new discrete data set. This is shown in Figure 3.2(c). The dotted lines are the newly interpolated sample points. To reconstruct the continuous function we need to apply an interpolation filter to the original voxels in the data set. Several different interpolation filters can be used to do that. This will be explained in Chapter 5.

To calculate the gradient, we add one more step to this process. After reconstructing the continuous function, we first compute its derivative and then resample the derivative function, instead of the function itself. This is shown in Figure 3.2(d). This intuitively makes sense, because the derivative is a measure of how quickly the continuous function changes. That is exactly what we need to know when calculating the gradient.

Now we know the theory behind gradient computation, but how do we actually calculate a gradient given a data set? There are several different methods, each with its own advantages and disadvantages, just as for interpolation. The next section will discuss one commonly used method. Later in this chapter we will discuss some alternatives.

The Central Difference Gradient Estimator

The gradient can be calculated using several different methods, just like interpolation. Some commonly used interpolation methods are linear interpolation, nearest neighbor, bicubic, and so on. The central difference gradient estimator is a commonly used operator. It is not necessarily the best operator in terms of quality, but it is fast and easy to implement. Later in this chapter we will discuss additional gradient operators and go into detail regarding quality and performance trade-offs.

The central difference gradient estimator is defined as follows:

$$D_x = f(x - 1,y,z) - f(x + 1,y,z)$$
$$D_y = f(x,y - 1,z) - f(x,y + 1,z) \qquad (3.3)$$
$$D_z = f(x,y,z - 1) - f(x,y,z + 1)$$

Where $f(x,y,z)$ is the value of the voxel at position (x,y,z) in the data set. D_x, D_y, and D_z are the components of the three-dimensional gradient vector:

$$D = [D_x, D_y, D_z] \qquad (3.4)$$

As you can see from Equation (3.3) and Figure 3.3 the central difference gradient estimator is a simple subtraction in each of the

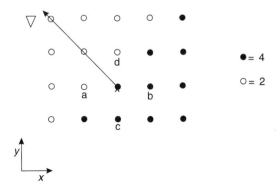

FIGURE 3.3 Two-dimensional example. The central difference gradient operator results in a vector of $(a\text{-}b,\ c\text{-}d) = (-2,2)$.

directions of the major axis of the data set. Since it consists of only subtractions, it is easy to implement both in software and hardware and is relatively fast. However it is not a very accurate estimator. There are better ones. This operator is sometimes also referred to as the six-point operator, since it needs six voxels to compute.

A different way to write the central difference gradient estimator is as a convolution kernel. Since the operator is the same in the x-, y-, and z-axis, we can get away with writing a one-dimensional kernel:

$$D_{x,y,z} = \begin{bmatrix} -1 & 0 & 1 \end{bmatrix} \qquad\qquad (3.5)$$

This is exactly the same as Equation (3.3). It is just a different notation, one you will sometimes find in the literature.

We now know why the gradient is important and how to calculate the gradient using the central difference method. The next section discusses what we do with the gradient information in volume rendering.

What Is the Gradient Used For in Volume Rendering?

The gradient is used in two places in the volume rendering pipeline. It is used in the shading part of the pipeline, and it may be used in the classification stage of the pipeline. Classification is the topic of the next chapter. The rest of this chapter will discuss shading and lighting.

In conventional computer graphics, a surface normal is needed to shade a pixel of a polygon that is rendered. This surface normal is used in a Gouraud or Phong shading model, together with other information like the position of the light sources, their color, and the material properties assigned to the polygon. The whole purpose of this is to make the scene that is being rendered look as real as possible. In volume rendering we do not have a surface normal available, since in general we do not know where a surface is in a data set. Instead we replace the surface normal in the illumination model with the gradient. The shading stage in the volume rendering pipeline applies a Phong illumination model to each voxel in the data set. It therefore needs to know the gradient at each voxel position. The Phong illumination model will be explained later in this chapter. First we will discuss additional gradient operators.

MORE GRADIENT OPERATORS

Research has shown that accurate gradient estimation is one of the most important factors that determines the look and quality of a volume rendered image. One of the results of this research is that it is better to use an accurate gradient filter than it is to use an accurate interpolation filter, if such a trade-off has to be made. Intuitively this makes sense, since the gradient is an essential component of the illumination model, and that is key to the visual understanding of the final rendered image. Also the gradient can optionally be used in the classification stage. This means that the gradient has a major impact on the rendering. Therefore it is important to be able to estimate it accurately.

Gradient operators are three-dimensional filters. As such we can apply conventional signal processing theory and filter design techniques to come up with new and better filters. In the For Further Study section you will find several references to papers that do exactly that. Filter design is a whole science of its own and not the topic of this book. However we will use some basic filtering concepts to discuss different gradient operators.

Sobel Operator

Instead of using six voxels for the central difference to estimate the gradient, an obvious choice is to use all 26 voxels that surround one voxel in 3D space. This is also referred to as 26-point neighborhood operators. These operators are usually a better estimation of the gradient, but the downside is that they are computationally more expensive. Another disadvantage can be that some additional smoothing is introduced in the rendering, but that depends on the specific gradient operator. However there are some very good 26-point neighborhood operators, and the three-dimensional Sobel operator is one of them.

In 1968 Irwin Sobel developed a two-dimensional edge, or gradient, operator. This operator became well known in the image processing field under the name Sobel operator. Sobel extended the ideas he applied to construct his two-dimensional operator to three dimensions, resulting in the following gradient operator (see Figure 3.4). This figure shows a 3 × 3 × 3 convolution kernel as a series of

$$x = -1$$
$$\begin{bmatrix} -2 & 0 & 2 \\ -3 & 0 & 3 \\ -2 & 0 & 2 \end{bmatrix}$$

$$x = 0$$
$$\begin{bmatrix} -3 & 0 & 3 \\ -6 & 0 & 6 \\ -3 & 0 & 3 \end{bmatrix}$$

$$x = 1$$
$$\begin{bmatrix} -2 & 0 & 2 \\ -3 & 0 & 3 \\ -3 & 0 & 3 \end{bmatrix}$$

FIGURE 3.4   Three-dimensional Sobel gradient operator. The 3x3x3 kernel for the z-direction is shown.

three 3×3 kernels. To get the x-component of the gradient vector, the $3 \times 3 \times 3$ convolution kernel in Figure 3.4 has to be applied to all 26 voxels around the voxel at which we want to know the gradient. To get the y- and z-components of the gradient vector we will need to rotate the kernel in Figure 3.4 so it aligns with the y- and z-axes, respectively, and apply the $3 \times 3 \times 3$ kernel two more times. Thus in total we will have to do 54 multiplies (3×18) and 51 (3×17) additions to compute one gradient vector. That is a lot of computation if you consider that a data set might have tens of millions of voxels in it, and you will have to do 54 multiplies and 51 additions for each voxel.

A very nice property of this gradient operator is that it is nearly isotropic. That means that the result of the operator does not depend on the orientation of a structure or boundary in the data set. The central difference gradient operator is not isotropic (see Figure 3.5). As you can see in Figure 3.5(a) the magnitude of the gradient using central difference is 1. In Figure 3.5(b) we still use the central difference operator, but the orientation of the boundary in the data is at a 45-degree angle with respect to Figure 3.5(a). As you can see the magnitude has now increased to $\sqrt{2}$. Thus the magnitude of the gradient changes with the orientation of the boundary. That can be

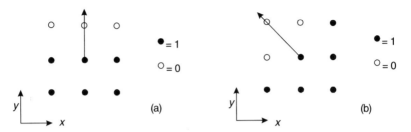

FIGURE 3.5 Two-dimensional situation. The white dots are voxels with an intensity of zero, the black dots are voxels with an intensity of 1. (a) The central difference gradient operator results in the gradient vector [0,1] and a magnitude of 1; (b) now the central difference operator results in a gradiant vector of [−1,1] and a magnitude of √2.

a disadvantage, especially in the classification stage where the magnitude of the gradient is used to assign opacities to voxels.

Intermediate Difference Operator

A computationally simple gradient operator is the intermediate difference operator. It is a surprisingly good one, given its simplicity. Its convolution kernel, in one dimension, is

$$D_{x,y,z} = [-1 \quad 1] \tag{3.6}$$

This is very similar to the central difference. The voxel where the gradient is computed is used in the computation (see Figure 3.6). This figure shows a one-dimensional example. Four voxels are shown with alternating intensities. Since the intermediate difference subtracts two voxel intensities right next to each other, it will be better able to register very fast changing data than the central difference can. For example, suppose that in Figure 3.6 voxels B and D have an intensity value of 100 and voxels A and C an intensity value of zero. Applying the central difference operator to voxels B and C will result in a gradient of zero. This is wrong since the data is changing rapidly, and there should thus be a gradient. On the other hand, if we apply the intermediate difference operator to voxels B and C, we get a gradient of 100 and −100 at points k and l, respectively, which is what you would expect. As you can see the central difference always calculates the gradient right at a voxel. The intermediate difference calculates the gradient right in between

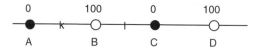

FIGURE 3.6 One-dimensional gradient example. Black voxels A and C have intensity values of 0, the white voxels B and D have intensity of 100. The k and l positions denote where the gradients computed with the intermediate gradient method fall.

two voxels. In order to get the gradient at the sample point we will need to interpolate the gradients with, for example, linear interpolation, or cubic interpolation.

The images in Figure 3.7 illustrate the difference between a rendering using the central difference gradient operator [Figure 3.7(a)] and a rendering using the intermediate difference gradient operator [Figure 3.7(b)]. Figure 3.7(b) shows the ability of the intermediate difference operator to register small features in a data set. Small features mean that data is changing rapidly in a small neighborhood of voxels. For example, the small holes in the left side of the skull behind the eye socket are not visible in Figure 3.7(a). The image in Figure 3.7(a) is somewhat smoother than the one in Figure 3.7(b). The central difference operator is a low-pass filter which introduces smoothing.

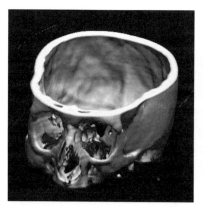
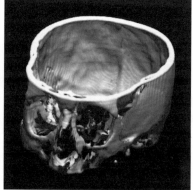

a   b

FIGURE 3.7 (a) Rendering of a CT skull data set using the central difference gradient operator; (b) same rendering using intermediate difference gradient operator. (Data set courtesy of the Mayo Clinic.)

GOURAUD AND PHONG SHADING

In computer graphics literature you will quite often encounter the terms Phong and Gouraud shading or illumination. Henri Gouraud in 1971 and Bui Tuong Phong in 1975 both developed techniques to make geometric models rendered on a computer look more realistic. The terms Phong and Gouraud shading refer to two different shading models applied to polygons. The Gouraud model is the computationally simpler of the two. Both shading models can use a Phong illumination model. This is somewhat confusing, since the name Phong applies both to a shading and illumination model. We will first discuss the Phong illumination model and then go into the difference between the two shading models.

The Phong Illumination Model

First a note about illumination models in general. The goal of an illumination model is to simulate the reflection of light of a surface, and the effect it has on the color that you as an observer perceive while looking at that surface. For example, picture a black bowling ball. Now picture a white light shining on the bowling ball. You will see the reflection of the light in the bowling ball, and the color you see is not black any longer. It will be close to white. These are the effects an illumination model tries to describe. Another goal of designing an illumination model is to make this model simple, so it can be computed efficiently. Historically when illumination models were developed, physical correctness was not much of a concern. It was not that important to correctly model the physics and optics behind illumination, shading, shadows, and so on, but rather emphasis was and is on efficient computation.

The Phong illumination model describes the effects of ambient light as well as diffuse and specular reflection of light that illuminates a surface. For each point on the surface we will have to evaluate the illumination model. Thus an illumination model is point-based. We will briefly discuss the ambient, diffuse, and specular components of the Phong model.

Ambient Light. An ambient light source is a light with the same intensity everywhere in the scene that is being rendered. It does not depend on the angle of the light with respect to the surface. It is nondirectional light source. We can describe the color of a surface when an ambient light illuminates it as follows:

$$C_o = C_a k_a O_d \qquad (3.7)$$

Here C_o is the resulting color after an ambient light with color C_a illuminates a point on an object. k_a is a material property called the ambient reflection coefficient. It is a number between 0 and 1. It is an easy way to describe different materials in a scene. For example a black object will absorb more light than a white object, and therefore its ambient reflection coefficient will be close to zero. O_d is the diffuse color of the point on an object. Of course you will have to apply the above equation three times: once for each color component, red, green, and blue.

Diffuse Reflection.   Diffuse reflection accounts for a point light source in a scene that radiates uniformly in all directions. The color of a point on a surface will depend on the distance of the point to the light source and the orientation of the surface to the light source. Often the distance of the light source to the surface is not taken into account. That amounts to saying the light source is positioned infinitely far away. In this case the point light source is called a *directional light.* Thus the only extra parameter we need to take into account, over the ambient light model, is the angle between the surface and the light source.

The orientation of a surface can be described by its normal N at the point that is being shaded. The vector that points from that point on the surface to the light source is called L. For a directional light, L is constant. The angle between L and N is θ (see Figure 3.8). N and L are the normalized versions of L and N. This is important. If they are not normalized, you will have to normalize them first before applying the illumination model. The Phong illumination model with diffuse reflection now becomes

$$C_o = C_a k_a O_d + C_p k_d O_d \cos \theta \qquad (3.8)$$

As you can see, we added a new term to the ambient term. C_p is the color of the point light source. k_d is the diffuse reflection coef-

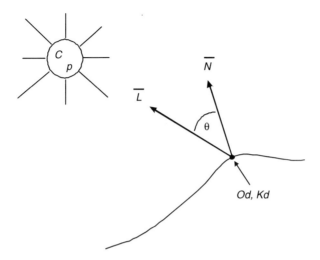

FIGURE 3.8 Diffuse reflection situation. The color assigned to a point on the surface depends only on the angle between the light vector and the surface normal.

ficient, analog to the ambient reflection coefficient. θ is the angle between the light source vector and the surface normal. As you can see from the second term in Equation (3.8), if the angle is 90 degrees, $\cos\theta = 0$ and there is no diffuse reflection that contributes to the illumination. On the other hand if the angle is 0 degrees, the contribution is maximal, because now $\cos\theta = 1$. This model is only valid if the angle between $\overline{L}$ and $\overline{N}$ ranges from 0 to 90 degrees. If the angle is bigger than 90 degrees, there is no diffuse reflection contribution. You can think of this situation as if the surface is being lit from the other side, the back face.

Since $\overline{L}$ and $\overline{N}$ are normalized, we can apply some mathematics which eliminates the need for us to figure out what the angle θ between the two vectors is. Mathematics tells us that the dot product between $\overline{L}$ and $\overline{N}$ equals $\cos\theta$. This only works if $\overline{L}$ and $\overline{N}$ are normalized. We now have the following illumination model:

$$C_o = C_a k_a O_d + C_p k_d O_d (\overline{N} \cdot \overline{L}) \tag{3.9}$$

Note that we have to apply Equation (3.9) three times, one time for each color component, red, green, and blue.

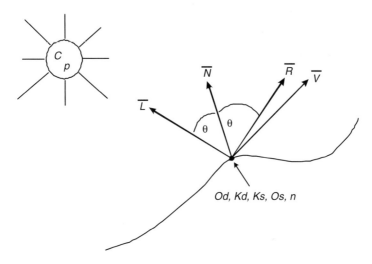

FIGURE 3.9 Specular reflection situation. The color assigned to a point on the surface also depends on the angle between the reflection vector and the viewer.

Specular Reflection. The specular reflection term in the illumination model we are building accounts for shiny highlights in a rendering. Do you remember the example of the bowling ball? The shiny white spot on the bowling ball is due to specular reflection. The fact that you see the rest of the bowling ball at all is due to the ambient and diffuse part of the illumination model. Specular reflection is fairly localized. Its intensity falls off fairly sharply around the reflection point. How fast it falls off is controlled with the specular reflection exponent n. For a perfect reflector, like a mirror, n would be infinity and you see only the specular reflection if your eye is exactly in line with the reflected light. Often specular reflection doesn't depend on the color of the surface at all, it is assumed that the color you will perceive is always white. Sometimes you will see illumination models with a separate specular color O_s as its color. The full Phong illumination model now is

$$C_o = C_a k_a O_d + C_p [k_d O_d (\overline{N} \cdot \overline{L}) + k_s O_s (\overline{R} \cdot \overline{V})^n] \qquad (3.10)$$

As you can see we did not add a light source; we only added some terms to model what happens when a point light source illuminates a surface (see also Figure 3.9). k_s is the specular reflection coefficient and is a material property. $\overline{R}$ is the (normalized) reflection vector. It is the direction light would reflect if shone upon a perfect mirror. In other words, it is the light vector $\overline{L}$ mirrored about the normal $\overline{N}$. $\overline{V}$ is the vector from the point to be shaded toward you, the viewer. The dot product between $\overline{R}$ and $\overline{V}$ accounts for the fact that you are not always looking directly into the reflection, that is, that $\overline{R}$ and $\overline{V}$ are not exactly aligned. To create a sharper cutoff the result of the dot product is raised to the power of n, the specular reflection exponent.

There is much more to be said about illumination and shading. Please refer to the For Further Study section for more information. Topics we did not discuss, mainly because they are not important in volume rendering, are light source attenuation, spotlights, physically based illumination models, and so on.

DIFFERENCE BETWEEN GOURAUD AND PHONG SHADING

Both shading models, Gouraud and Phong, typically apply the Phong illumination model from Equation (3.10), or some close derivative. The difference lies in when and where the illumination model is applied.

First we will discuss the polygonal case. When shading a geometric model consisting of polygons, normals are typically known at the vertices of a polygon (see Figure 3.10). These normals are used to apply a Phong illumination model to the vertices. This results in a color at each vertex. After doing that there are two different ways to proceed.

Gouraud shading will take the colors at the vertices, resulting from the illumination, and interpolate these colors across the edges of the polygon and across the scan lines. This is shown in Figure 3.11(a). Typically linear interpolation is used, but any interpolation method can be applied. The color at point J is interpolated from the colors RGB_1 and RGB_2. The color at point K is interpolated from the colors RGB_1 and RGB_3. Next the colors at the pixels on the scan line are interpolated from the colors at the points J and K. After one scan line is processed, you will have to do the next scan line until the whole triangle is scan converted.

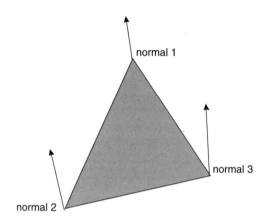

FIGURE 3.10   A polygon with normals at each of the vertices.

Phong shading will take the normals at the vertices and will in-terpolate these normals across the edges of the polygon and across the scan lines [see Figure 3.11(b)]. The normal at points *J* and *K* are computed by interpolating the normals at the vertices. Then these normals, at points *J* and *K*, are interpolated across the scan line and a Phong illumination model is applied to each pixel on the scan line. This is a more accurate way of shading a polygon since the il-

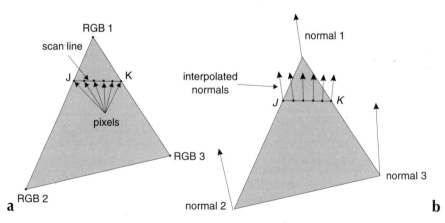

FIGURE 3.11   (a) Gouraud shading. Colors are interpolated across edges and scanlines. (b) Phong shading. Normals are interpolated across edges and across scan lines.

lumination model is applied to every point on that polygon, instead of interpolating the colors at the vertices. However, the Phong shading model is much more computationally intensive than the Gouraud model, not only because the illumination model has to be applied more often, but also because the interpolated normals need to be normalized. Although the normals at the vertices are normalized, the interpolated ones in general are not normalized any more. Normalization is a compute-intensive operation.

Using Shading in Volume Rendering

In volume rendering we can make a similar distinction between Phong and Gouraud shading as was done for polygonal rendering in the previous section. When do we interpolate and when do we apply an illumination model in the volume rendering pipeline? The volume rendering pipeline we discussed in Chapter 1 shows that the interpolation stage happens first, then the classification and shading stages. This means that we interpolate the voxel intensities and normals at the voxel positions down to the sample points and use the interpolated intensity and normal in the Phong illumination model. This is Phong shading in volume rendering [see Figure 3.12(a)].

On the other hand we can shade and classify voxels first and thus assign a RGB value to each voxel and then interpolate these RGB values to the sample points. This is Gouraud shading in volume rendering [see Figure 3.12(b)]. We calculate the normal at the voxel position and use that normal in the Phong illumination model to generate RGB values, which we then interpolate.

In this book we use a Phong shading model. Thus we interpolate normals and then calculate the colors. Since we are also compositing the colors of each sample point to get the final pixel color, it is not easy to predict what the result of changing a parameter of the lighting model will be. The final rendered image can change drastically when a parameter of the illumination model is only modified slightly. This is because compositing is a nonlinear operation.

Since it is hard to predict what will happen with our illumination model, we will try to keep it simple. Also, the main goal of

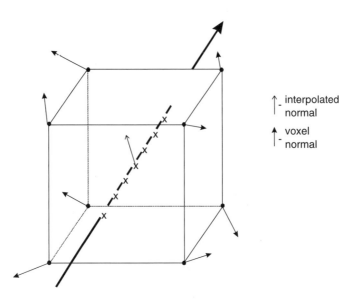

FIGURE 3.12(a) Phong shading in volume rendering. Each voxel has a normal, which is interpolated down to the sample points on the ray.

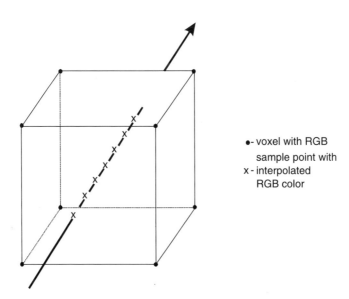

FIGURE 3.12(b) Gouraud shading in volume rendering. Each voxel has a color, which is interpolated down to the sample points on the ray.

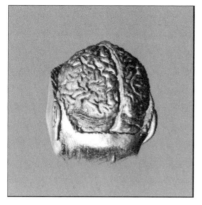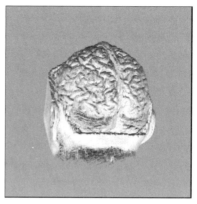

a b

FIGURE 3.13 Rendering with ambient and diffuse reflection components only: (a) Rendering with one light source; (b) rendering with two light sources.

shading is to enhance the visual understanding of the data set, not necessarily to achieve photo realism. Typically it is enough to use one or two white light sources placed at infinity and a Phong illumination model. Sometimes the Phong model will not even have a specular component. See Figures 3.13, 3.14, and 3.15 for a comparison. These figures shows six renderings of the University of North Carolina Chapel Hill brain data set. Figures 3.13(a), 3.14(a) and 3.15(a) are rendered using one light source. Figures 3.13(b),

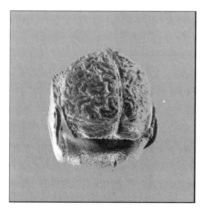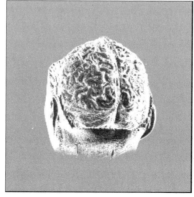

a b

FIGURE 3.14 Rendering with ambient and specular reflection components only: (a) Rendering with one light source; (b) rendering with two light sources.

 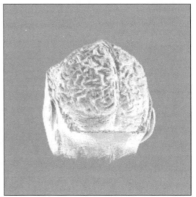

a   b

FIGURE 3.15 Rendering with ambient, diffuse, and specular reflection components: (a) Rendering with one light source; (b) rendering with two light sources.

3.14(b), and 3.15(b) are rendered using two light sources. In Figures 3.13(a) and (b) the Phong illumination model has an ambient and diffuse component and no specular component. In Figures 3.14(a) and (b) there is an ambient and a specular component, but no diffuse component in the illumination model. Figures 3.15(a) and (b) are rendered with a full Phong illumination model, with an ambient, diffuse, and specular component. Figure 3.13 shows, in our opinion, the best renderings. Figures 3.14(a) and (b) almost look like negatives. A diffuse component in the illumination model is highly desirable. Figures 3.15(a) and (b) are flat, washed out. We do not show a rendering with only an ambient term in the illumination model, but the result is a flat, white image.

FOR FURTHER STUDY

Gradient operators are filters. As such a lot of information can be found in the signal processing literature. Since gradient operators are a derivative of an interpolation function, it pays to study interpolation filters as well. Good papers on interpolation filters are [40], [116], [187], [191], [145], [158], [27], [154], [165], and [156]. If you are mostly interested in an overview of interpolation filters, check out [187] and [158]. [27], [154], and [165] evaluate interpolation filters specifically for use in volume rendering.

Several good papers on gradient filtering in volume rendering are [129], [192], [76], [156], [265], and [17]. General edge detection and gradient filtering information can be found in [202], [147], and [260]. The Sobel operator is described in [184] and [44]. The derivation of the 3D Sobel operator is not officially published.

Shading and Illumination are discussed in depth in [65]. This is a standard work about computer graphics, and worth buying. The original Gouraud illumination paper is [77] and the original Phong illumination paper is [182].

CHAPTER

4

CLASSIFICATION

Classification and shading, discussed in the previous chapter, are the two critical operations in volume rendering. The classification step in the volume rendering pipeline lets you find structures in a data set without explicitly defining the shape and extent of that structure. It allows you to see inside an object and explore its structures instead of only visualizing the surface of that object. This is a powerful part of volume rendering, and one of the main reasons volume rendering is so useful. Compare this to surface rendering techniques which involves a preprocessing step to decide if a surface is present or not in the data set before you can do the rendering. This yes/no decision is prone to errors. If the decision is made in the preprocessing step that there is a surface somewhere, but in reality there is not, the rendering will show a faulty representation of the data set.

On the other hand, the classification step in volume rendering is far more sophisticated than a simple binary decision process. If there is a structure in a data set, it can be made visible with classification. The classification stage does this by assigning a new property, called opacity, to each voxel in the data set. The opacity is a measure for how translucent that voxel is. It is a number between 0 and 1 that describes how much light that falls on a voxel will be absorbed by that voxel. It tells you how easy it is to see through that voxel. Assigning an opacity to a voxel can be a very complex oper-

ation and is the topic of the next section. The important thing to remember is that classification allows you, the user, to bring out structures in a data set by assigning the voxels in the structure a high
opacity, thus making the structure visible. Conversely it makes
structures of little interest transparent.

Before we go on and explain transfer functions, we will introduce histograms. Histograms are typically used in imaging applications, but they are also a very useful tool in designing or choosing a
transfer function for a data set.

HISTOGRAMS

A histogram tells you how many times a voxel (or pixel) of a certain
value is present in the data set. A histogram is a plot with the voxel
(or pixel) values on the horizontal axis and the number of occur-
rences, or frequency, on the vertical axis (see Figure 4.1). A histogram gives you information about the spread of all possible voxel
(or pixel) values. Why is this useful? Knowing something about the
spread of the voxel intensities can help you decide which classification transfer function to use. Transfer functions are the topic of the
next section. It is important to realize that almost any image, or data
set, will have noise in it. Noise is inherent in sampled data. The data
sets you are typically dealing with are acquired by some kind of
scanner, as described in Chapter 1, which will produce noise. Some
will produce more noise than others. For example, an ultrasound
scanner produces very noisy images, while a CT scanner can produce crisp high-resolution data sets. In-depth discussion of noise is
outside the scope of this book. However you should be aware of the
fact that it will show up in a histogram, and you should either try to
filter it out, or if that is not possible, consider it in the interpretation
of your rendering.

TRANSFER FUNCTIONS

Classification is the process of assigning an opacity value to a voxel.
This assignment is some function of the properties of a voxel, like its
intensity, or its local gradient magnitude. This function is called the

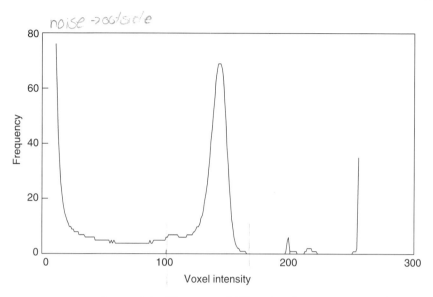

FIGURE 4.1   Histogram of CT engine data set.

opacity transfer function. Remember, classification will allow you to bring out certain features in a data set, or make them completely transparent. The opacity transfer function can have any number of voxel properties as its input, but most typically it is only a function of a voxel's intensity, or sometimes a function of the voxel's intensity and the local gradient magnitude. Thus in formula form

$$\alpha_1 = O(I_{i'}|\nabla_i|,...,...,...)$$

where $O(...)$ is the opacity transfer function, and $|\nabla|$ the local gradient magnitude. To make all this clearer we will start with a simple example.

In Figure 4.2 and Plate 6 you see a volume rendering of a CT data set. This is an engine block. If we look at the histogram of the original data set, Figure 4.1, we see that in a CT data set there are distinct ranges of voxel intensities. The peak all the way to the left is noise. It is the empty space outside the engine block. If we set the opacity transfer function so that only voxels with intensities between 100 and 170 are assigned a high opacity number, say 0.9, we get the rendering in Figure 4.2(a). The transfer function is shown in Figure 4.2(b). As you can see, we selected the outside of the en-

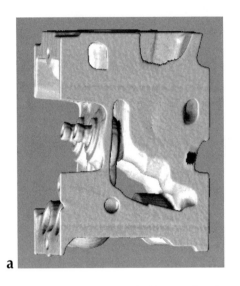 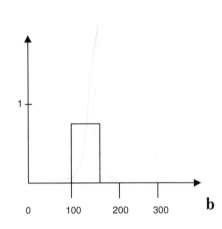

a   b

0   100   200   300

FIGURE 4.2 (a) Outer shell is rendered opaque; (b) the transfer function that generated (a).

gine. If, on the other hand, we do the same but with voxels in the intensity range between 185 and 235, we get Figure 4.3(a) (see also Plate 7). Now we selected the inner parts of the engine, plus a plate at the back. Apparently there are at least two different materials in this engine block. We can also make the outer parts of the engine semitransparent and the inside opaque. This is shown in Figure 4.4(a) and Plate 8. We did this by assigning a low opacity value to the voxels in the range 100 to 170 and a high opacity to the voxels in the intensity range 185 and 235. Of course this shows only one possible rendering. By changing the transfer function you can make the outer parts of the engine more or less transparent. This is a very powerful feature of volume rendering.

The previous example used only the voxel intensity to classify the data set. This is fine for a CT data set where it is easy to identify distinct ranges of voxel values. Often things are not so clear-cut. In an MRI data set of the human body for example, the same voxel intensity can be assigned to parts of the skin as to the brain. Simple classification based on only the voxel intensity will fail in this case. Therefore it is useful to use more information for your classification.

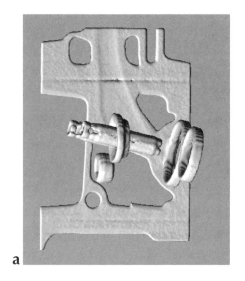

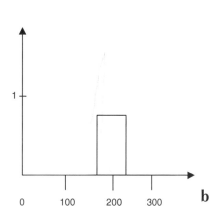

a

b

FIGURE 4.3 (a) The backplate and inner parts of the engine block consist of a different material; (b) the transfer function that generated (a).

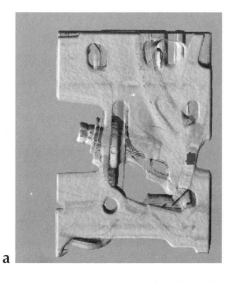

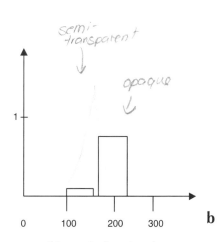

a

b

FIGURE 4.4 Outer shell rendered partially transparent; (b) transfer function that generated (a).

In the literature you will find examples where the local gradient magnitude is also used for classification. Remember, as we explained in Chapter 3, the gradient is a measure of how quickly data changes and in what direction. Thus a big gradient means that there is a rapid change of data, probably some boundary between two materials of some sort. This might be the boundary between rock and oil in a seismic data set, or the boundary between skin and bone in a medical data set.

The next example shows why it is sometimes useful to use gradient information in the classification stage of the volume rendering pipeline. Figure 4.5 shows different renderings of a seismic data set. This data set is acquired by a geological survey of some layers of the earth. In Figure 4.5(a) you can see the layers quite clearly. You can also see that there is a breakline: Layers are offset from each other in the vertical direction. In Figure 4.5(c) you see a rendering of the same layers but with different classification parameters. Both figures are classified using voxel intensities only. In Figure 4.5(c) we tried to visualize only the light-gray shaded layers in Figure 4.5(a). Figures 4.5(b) and 4.5(d), however, were classified using both the gradient magnitude and the voxel intensities. You can clearly see that layers in the earth come out much better in Figures 4.3(b) and 4.3(d).

How were these renderings generated? We used a block transfer function based on intensities only for Figures 4.5(a) and 4.5(c). For Figures 4.5(b) and 4.5(d) we used a transfer function that was originally published in Levoy's 1988 paper. See the For Further Study section for more information. This transfer function is shown in Figure 4.6.

This classification function was specifically designed to do very well at displaying iso surface values, that is, finding all the voxels in a data set that have a certain constant intensity value. However the gradient magnitude is also a measure for a boundary, or surface. Therefore this classification function combines the gradient magnitude with the voxel intensities to assign a high opacity to voxels that lie on or close to a surface, or a rapidly changing section of the data set.

If you look at Figure 4.6, you will see that both the gradient magnitude and the voxel intensity are used. The voxel intensities

intensity

intensity +
local gradient

different classification
parameter

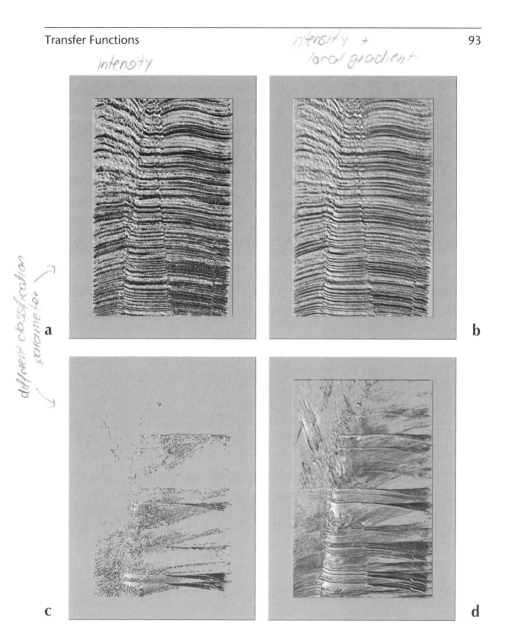

a

b

c

d

FIGURE 4.5 (a) Classification based on intensity only; (b) classification based on intensity and local gradient magnitude; (c) classification based on intensity only; (d) classification based on intensity and local gradient magnitude. (Data set courtesy of Srinivas Manapragada, Landmark Graphics.)

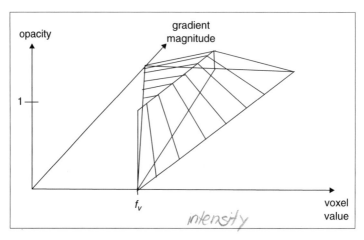

FIGURE 4.6 Classification function to emphasize surfaces and rapidly changing data.

are on the x-axis, the gradient magnitude on the y-axis, and the resulting opacity is on the z-axis. You position this classification
function, which we call "the tent," at the voxel intensity you are
interested in, f_v. All the voxels with intensity value f_v will get a high
opacity assigned, as well as all the voxels around f_v that also have
a significant gradient magnitude. The bigger the gradient magnitude, the further away a voxel's intensity can be from f_v. This classification function has two parameters: f_v and the parameter r
which is the maximum a voxel's intensity can deviate from f_v and
still get some opacity bigger than zero assigned. The formula for
this function is

$$\alpha_i\,(r,f_v) = 1 - \frac{1}{r|\nabla_i|}\,|f_v - I_i|\quad if\,|\nabla_i| > 0 \ and \ I_i - r|\nabla_i| \leq f_v \leq I_i + r|\nabla_i|$$

$$\alpha_i\,(r,f_v) = 1\qquad\qquad\qquad\quad if\,|\nabla_i| = 0$$

$$\alpha_i\,(r,f_v) = 0\qquad\qquad\qquad\quad otherwise$$

where $|\nabla_i|$ is the gradient magnitude at voxel i with intensity I_i
and $\alpha_i(r,f_v)$ is the opacity at voxel i. Note that if $f_v = I_i$, then
$\alpha_i(r,f_v) = 1$.

The previous examples make it clear that it is important to
choose the right classification function. Unfortunately we cannot

give you one universal rule for which one to use. The classification function you will want to use depends on the type of data you are trying to visualize. A histogram is a useful tool to aid in the selection of a classification function. If the volume rendering application you are using is able to render a data set in real time, you can interactively change the classification function, see the result of this change, and visually select one you like.

COLORING AND SHADING

It can be useful to use color in the rendering of a data set. Most data sets do not have intrinsic color values assigned to the voxels, only intensities. Therefore we have to come up with some mapping of the voxel intensity to an RGB color. This process is called *shading* in the volume rendering pipeline. If you are familiar with conventional computer graphics, this name is confusing. In conventional computer graphics shading means applying a shading model to the pixels that make up a primitive. In volume rendering, shading breaks down into two steps. First the voxel intensities are converted into a color; then a shading model is applied to these colors. We call the former process *coloring*. Shading models are discussed in the previous chapter.

Coloring is very much like classification. It is the process of turning voxel intensities into colors, with the goal of enhancing the visual understanding of the data set. We use three transfer functions to do coloring, one transfer function each for red, green, and blue:

$$R_i = T_r (I_i, ...)$$
$$G_i = T_g (I_i, ...)$$
$$B_i = T_b (I_i, ...)$$

where T_r, T_g, and T_b are the transfer functions for the colors red, green, and blue, respectively. These three transfer functions can be different from each other. If they were the same, you would generate a gray scale image. Typically they are only a function of the voxel intensity, but there is nothing that prevents you from defining a color transfer function that depends on intensities and the time of day, for example. It is important to realize that we are not trying to re-create reality as closely as possible. We are trying to enhance the rendering in such a way that it is easier to interpret. Figure 4.4, for example, was created by assigning red to the voxels in the intensity range 185 to 235. All the other voxels were colored white. The image is not purely red and white because we applied a Phong illumination model after the coloring step to all the voxels.

As you can see, choosing the right transfer functions is difficult. So far the most commonly used method to set transfer functions to explore a data set is trial and error. You repeatedly modify the transfer functions and evaluate the result, hoping the resulting rendering will be a good visualization which brings out some property of the data you are interested in. It is difficult to select transfer functions in a meaningful way. There are four transfer functions you will have to modify. The shading model, view direction, and compositing operation also affect the result of the rendering. Since there are so many parameters that influence the final rendering, it is hard to get an intuitive feeling about what will happen when you modify a transfer function even slightly. Also, different transfer functions may lead to interesting visualizations of different properties of the data. In Figure 4.7(a) and Plate 9 you see a rendering of a molecular structure generated by a quantum mechanics calculation of a one-electron orbital of a four-iron, eight-sulfur cluster which is found in many nat-

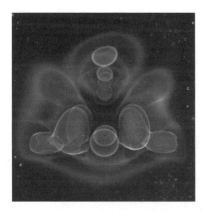
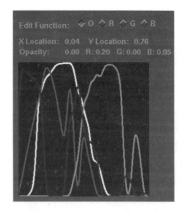

a   **b**

FIGURE 4.7 (a) Rendering of the high potential protein; (b) transfer functions used to generate (a). (Images courtesy of Hanspeter Pfister, Mitsubishi Electric Research Laboratory.)

ural proteins. The data set is commonly referred to in the literature as the high potential iron protein. In Figure 4.7(b) and Plate 10 you see a set of transfer functions for RGB and opacity (the white curve). These transfer functions were used to generate the image in Figure 4.7(a). As you can see, the shape of these transfer functions is not exactly intuitive. These transfer functions were chosen using a stochastic search technique, and not by simple trial and error. See the For Further Study section for more information about this technique.

SEGMENTATION

Classification and coloring are stages in the volume pipeline. Once you set up the transfer functions, classification and coloring will be executed automatically and repeated for every rendering of the data set. Although this is a very powerful feature of volume rendering, it has its limits. It is not possible to come up with transfer functions for each and every feature in a data set. If you are familiar with image processing, you know that there are countless sophisticated procedures and algorithms to do feature extraction, or character recognition, for example. Often these algorithms are semiautomatic and require some level of user interaction. This is the same in volume rendering. There are many researchers working on the problem of extracting, or segmenting, features in a data set. It is sometimes not possible to come up with an automatic algorithm that does the segmentation for you. The only option left is to label each voxel by hand. Or maybe you can design an algorithm that can work on its own most of the time, but needs some guidance once in a while. Whatever the algorithm, segmentation can be a time-consuming and difficult task. However, sometimes you will need to do this because it is simply not possible to come up with opacity and color transfer functions that will extract what you want to see.

We define segmentation as a labeling of voxels indicating material types. Thus a voxel is part of one material, or another. Segmentation is not continuous like classification.

Once you segmented the features you are interested in and labeled each voxel as belonging to a certain feature, you can store that labeling information with the data set and reuse it when necessary. Thus segmentation is a preprocessing step before you do the rendering. The volume rendering pipeline should use the labeling information you stored with the data set. That is where the classification and coloring transfer functions come into play again. Instead of having these transfer functions work on the voxel intensities, you will have them work on the labeling information. Remember that we said that these transfer functions can be a function of any voxel property. In this case that property is the labels attached to the voxels. If you do this you can come up with transfer functions that will assign different colors to different features, or different opacities to different features, or possibly both. The medical imaging industry is a great example of where they do this extensively.

We will look at three examples. In Figure 4.8(a) and Plate 11 you see a rendering of the University of North Carolina at Chapel Hill MRI brain data set. This data set can be downloaded for free from their Web site and is also available on the CD-ROM that

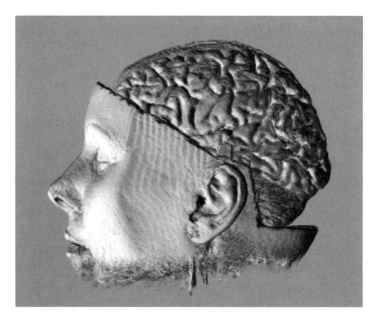

a

FIGURE 4.8   (a) Rendering without using segmentation information; (b) rendering using segmentation information and the same classification parameters as (a); (c) rendering using segmentation information. Skin and bone are made transparent in the classification stage.

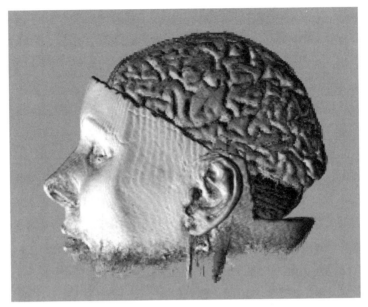

b

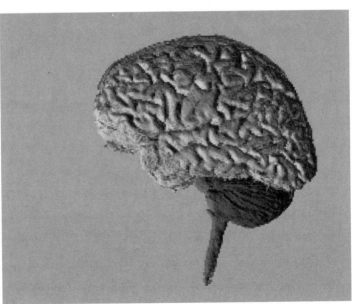

c

FIGURE 4.8 *Continued*

comes with this book. MRI data of the human body is hard to classify, since voxels with the same intensity typically belong to several different anatomical parts of the body. The only reason you see parts of the brain exposed in Figure 4.8(a) is because the bone of the skull in those places is not present in the original data set. We did not use segmentation information to render Figure 4.8(a). However, we did use segmentation information to generate Figure 4.8(b) (see also Plate 12). Here we labeled all the voxels in the data set and divided the voxels into four categories. We set up the coloring transfer functions so that the voxels get different colors assigned depending on their labels. The classification transfer function did not change

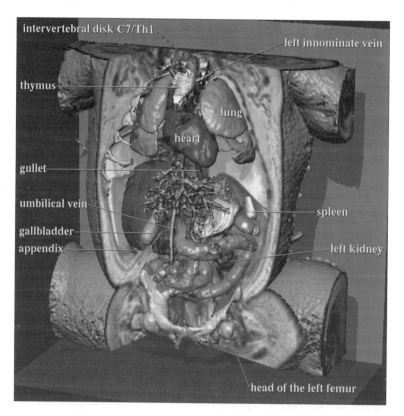

FIGURE 4.9 Volume rendering of a torso. Organs are labeled and rendered in different colors. (Image courtesy of the Institute of Math and Computer Science in Medicine, University of Hamburg.)

and is the same as the one used to render Figure 4.8(a). As you can see there are four different parts of the head rendered in different colors. The brown/gold color is the cerebral cortex, red is the cerebellum, blue the spinal cord, and gray is skin. In Figure 4.8(c) and Plate 13 we also changed the classification transfer function to make all the skin and bone in the data set transparent. Skin and bone have the same label, and therefore it is easy to assign an opacity of zero to those voxels while leaving the rest unchanged.

The next example also comes from the medical imaging discipline. In Figure 4.9 and Plate 14 you see a rendering of a torso. This image was generated by the University of Hamburg. This image is part of an effort where they constructed an atlas of the human body. They labeled each organ in the body, often by hand, while consulting surgeons to make sure they did it right. As you can see they extensively use the labeling information to color different organs.

The last example comes from the field of nondestructive testing. In Figure 4.10 and Plates 15 and 16 you see a CT scan of a sophisticated lock. Different parts are labeled, and this labeling information is used to set the transfer functions.

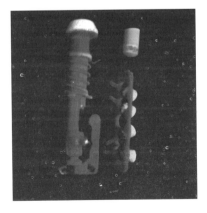

a   b

FIGURE 4.10 Volume rendering of a lock. Different parts are labeled. (a) Using the opacity transfer function the casing is made transparent; (b) casing is made visible and colored blue using the RGB transfer functions. (Data set courtesy of B. Schillinger. Images courtesy of Volume Graphics, GmbH, Germany.)

FOR FURTHER STUDY

In his 1988 paper Levoy [119] proposes two different classification functions. One of those we discussed earlier. This paper is worth reading, since it is probably the most referenced paper in volume rendering.

In [43] a more sophisticated method of classification and coloring is presented. Here the authors observe that it is possible for one voxel to be part of several different materials. For each material they assign a probability value to the voxel. This probability value indicates the percentage of the total voxel that contains that material. Each voxel has densities and color information for each material in that voxel. This method has the advantage of being able to represent the scanned object better and avoid aliasing artifacts because binary classification is avoided. However, rendering times will go up because there is more data to process, and assigning the probability values can be a very difficult problem.

A recent paper discussing transfer functions is [95]. This paper discusses stochastic methods to generate transfer functions. This approach is fundamentally different from the trial-and-error method, in that it defines objective measures for what the final rendering should be, like maximum image entropy or histogram variation. It then works backwards through the volume rendering pipeline to find the transfer functions that achieve those goals. Much improved results, by some of the same authors, can be found in [144].

Very little has been written about the transfer function selection process. We expect that this will change. Volume rendering systems are becoming more powerful and therefore interactive volume rendering a reality. With the availability of interactive systems, better methods for selection of transfer functions will become urgent.

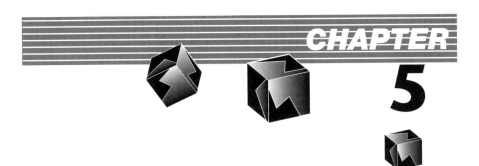

CHAPTER 5

INTERPOLATION

As we have seen, the fundamental concept of ray casting is to cast rays through our block of voxels. We then step along each ray, sampling and compositing the values to determine one final value to represent that ray. In Chapter 2, we discussed the mathematics behind stepping along the ray. First we find the initial point where the ray intersects our block of voxels. Then we traverse the ray, stepping small increments and resampling. Once the initial point is calculated, the next points are easily computed by adding Δx, Δy, and Δz. Figure 5.1 shows this traversal.

As we step along the ray sampling, more often than not, we need to sample between the voxels rather than right at a voxel. Figure 5.2 shows the need to resample in the middle of eight known values. Generating samples between voxels involves a weighted sum of the voxels that surround this sample point. New value generation using existing voxels is called interpolation.

INTERPOLATION KERNELS

There are a number of different interpolation methods. Each method is controlled by an interpolation kernel. The shape of the interpolation kernel provides the coefficients for the weighted interpolation

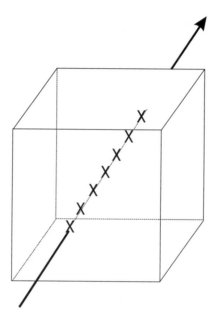

FIGURE 5.1   Stepping along the ray.

sum. Figure 5.3 shows the different interpolation kernels we will discuss in this chapter. The final image quality is highly dependent on which interpolation kernel you choose.

Interpolation kernels can be thought of as overlays. When a value needs to be interpolated, the kernel is placed on top of the known values. The kernel is centered at the interpolation point of interest. Everywhere the interpolation kernel intersects the position of a known value (voxel), the two values are multiplied.

Using Figure 5.4, we can go through an example. The values of our discrete function are $f[-1] = 0.4$, $f[0] = 1.05$, $f[1] = 0.9$, and $f[2] = 0.57$. The values of the interpolation function at these discrete points are -0.02, 0.38, 0.66, and -0.07. To interpolate the new value, multiply the corresponding values

$$0.4 \times -0.02 + 1.05 \times 0.38 + 0.9 \times 0.66 + 0.57 \times -0.07 = 0.945$$

Our newly interpolated value is 0.945.

The one-dimensional interpolation kernels can be applied to interpolate in two and three dimensions if the kernel is separable. A

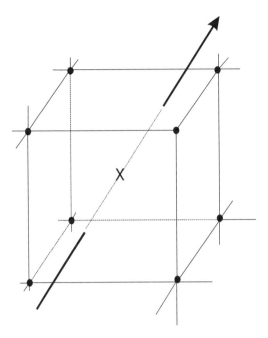

FIGURE 5.2 Sample point amid eight voxels.

two-dimensional function is considered separable if it can be decomposed as follows:

$$f(x,y) = g(x,y) \cdot h(x,y)$$

All interpolation kernels presented in this chapter are separable.

Interpolating values in three dimensions with separable kernels consists of three stages. In each stage, a one-dimensional interpolation is done with respect to one axis (x, y, or z). This is shown in Figure 5.5.

FIGURE 5.3 Different interpolation kernels.

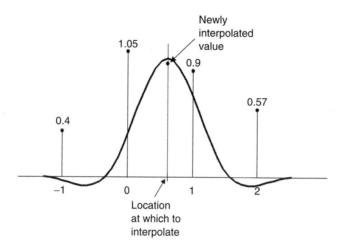

FIGURE 5.4   How interpolation is done.

In order to get the interpolated value at the point marked with an x in Figure 5.5(a) we first compute four one-dimensional interpolations in the x-direction. The results are the squares in Figure 5.5(b). Then we interpolate between those four squares in the y-direction, which results in two values shown by the circles in Figure 5.5(c). Finally we compute the last one-dimensional interpolation between the two circles, which results in the final value.

Nearest Neighbor

Interpolation via nearest neighbor is the simplest and crudest method. To put it simply, nearest neighbor looks for the value nearest the interpolation point and uses that value. From the shape of

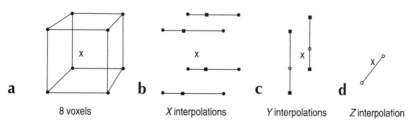

FIGURE 5.5   (a–d) Interpolation in three dimensions.

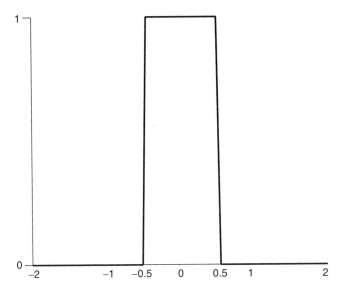

FIGURE 5.6   Nearest neighbor interpolation kernel.

the interpolation kernel in Figure 5.6, you can see that only one value is used in the process. It is more a selection process than the weighted sum used in typical interpolation. This was the interpolation method used in Chapter two.

Figure 5.7 shows how to apply this kernel to known values. Since the kernel has the width of one, it will use only one value.

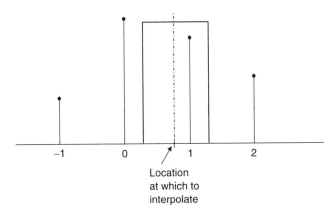

FIGURE 5.7   Interpolation via nearest neighbor.

The height of the kernel is 1, so the output of the interpolation is 1 times whatever value is within one unit of the point to be interpolated. In this example, it will be the value at location 1.

The closest sample can easily be selected with the following code:

flood(*address* + 0.5)

Figure 5.8 shows an example of nearest neighbor interpolation. The image has been magnified by factors of 4 and 15.

Nearest neighbor interpolation can suffer from severe artifacts. The blocky appearance in Figure 5.8(c) is called aliasing. Aliasing is the anomaly that occurs when a continuous function is sampled at too low a frequency. Those of you familiar with sampling theory, know of the Nyquist criterion. Simply put, a signal can be reconstructed if it is sampled at a rate equal to or higher than twice the highest frequency of the original signal. Figure 5.9 shows a simple example of sampling a signal at too low a frequency. The top line is a single scan line of an image. It is minified by a factor of three via simple subsampling. Viewing only the resulting sampled signal, you would assume the original sample is pure white. This is not the case. The sampled signal suffers from aliasing.

Another downfall of nearest neighbor interpolation is the shifting of images. The rounding nature of nearest neighbor interpolation can cause image shifts up to one-half of a pixel. This is an issue if image registration is needed in your application.

a, b   **c**

FIGURE 5.8   (a) Original image; (b) scaled by a factor of 4 via nearest neighbor interpolation; (c) scaled by a factor of 15 via nearest neighbor interpolation.

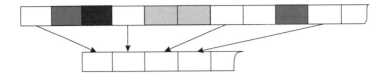

FIGURE 5.9   Minifying a scanline by a factor of 3 via subsampling. The resulting sample suffers from aliasing.

Despite these negatives, nearest neighbor interpolation is very easy to implement. Also because of the lower number of CPU cycles required, it can provide an interpolation method for a very responsive volume renderer.

Linear Interpolation

A popular interpolation technique is linear interpolation. When applied to a two-dimensional signal, it is called bilinear interpolation. When applied to a three-dimensional signal, it is called trilinear interpolation. Linear interpolation offers image quality much higher than that provided with nearest neighbor interpolation at a cost of being more computationally intensive. Linear interpolation assumes a linear relationship between the points to interpolate and the points that bound it. Figure 5.10 shows a line drawn between two points. Any value interpolated linearly will lie on the line drawn.

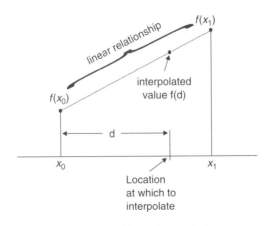

FIGURE 5.10   Linear Interpolation.

The interpolation formula is:

$$f(d) = \frac{f(x_1) - f(x_0)}{x_1 - x_0} \cdot d + f(x_0)$$

where d is the distance from the first sample x_0. In most cases, the sampling interval is equidistant and fixed at 1. When that is the case, the denominator becomes 1 and the equation is simplified. The corresponding interpolation kernel is shown in Figure 5.11.

Linear interpolation is easily extended to multiple dimensions. Figure 5.12 shows how interpolation is done in two dimensions. You begin with the four surrounding known values. The first two steps include interpolating points in the x-direction. The last step interpolates between these two points.

The same idea extends to three dimensions. We showed the general three-dimensional case in Figure 5.5. In the case of trilinear interpolation we compute two bilinear interpolations, one for the front face of the cube in Figure 5.5 and one for the back face. This results in the interpolated values in the y-direction [Figure 5.5(c)]. Next we compute one linear interpolation in the z-direction to get our result, as shown in Figure 5.5(d).

Figure 5.13 shows the results of interpolating via bilinear interpolation. The image quality is much better than that of nearest neighbor especially for large magnifications.

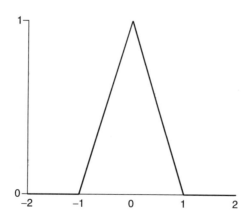

FIGURE 5.11   Linear interpolation kernel.

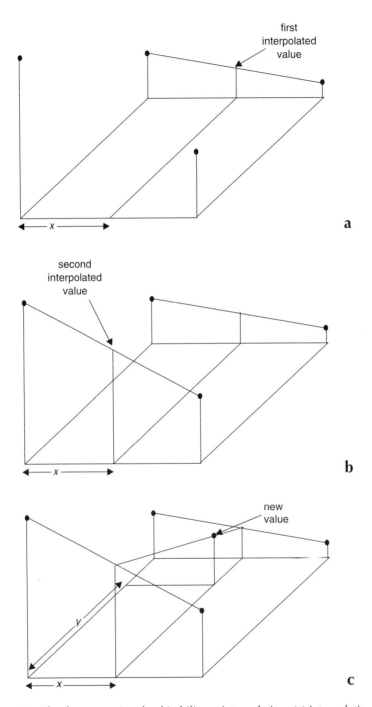

FIGURE 5.12 The three steps involved in bilinear interpolation: (a) Interpolation in the *x*-direction; (b) second interpolation in the *x*-direction; (c) last interpolation between the two previously interpolated points.

a, b   **c**

FIGURE 5.13 (a) Original image; (b) scaled by a factor of 4 via bilinear interpolation; (c) scaled by a factor of 15 via bilinear interpolation.

Bilinear interpolation suffers from its own artifacts. Although you cannot see them in Figure 5.13, you can see them in Figure 5.14. Figure 5.14(a) shows an image of a fruit arrangement. Figure 5.14(b) shows the results of scaling up one of the grapes. The white and black crosses that can be seen are a result of scaling an image with bilinear interpolation. One problem with bilinear interpolation is that it is not a radial interpolation kernel. The end result is a composite of an interpolation in the x-direction and then the y-direction. This creates the little white crosses. This anomaly is also seen when using trilinear interpolating. Despite these artifacts, linear interpolation is a step above nearest neighbor in terms of image quality.

a   **b**

FIGURE 5.14 (a) Original fruit image; (b) grape scaled up to show bilinear interpolation artifacts.

Cubic Convolution Interpolation

Cubic convolution interpolation is one step higher on the image quality scale than bilinear interpolation though it requires more computations. Figure 5.15 shows the interpolation kernels for cubic convolution interpolations. From Figure 5.11, you can see that the width of the linear interpolation kernel is 2 units. The width of the cubic convolution kernel is 4 units. Linear interpolation computes a new value using two sample points which requires two multiplications. Cubic convolution interpolation uses four sample points and therefore requires four multiplications in one dimension.

Cubic convolution interpolation introduces a new variable, a, which is used to control the sharpness of the kernel. You can see in Figure 5.15 that the more negative the value of a, the more negative the sided lobes and also the more sharpening you will see in your resulting data.

Because the kernel has negative side lobes, it is possible to interpolate negative values. This can be a problem, because negative voxel values often do not mean anything. Implementations of this interpolation method should check for negative output values and clamp them to 0 or rescale all values.

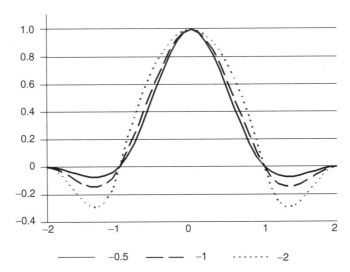

FIGURE 5.15 Cubic convolution interpolation kernel plotted for various a values.

The cubic convolution function is defined as

$$f(x) = \begin{cases} (a + 2)|x|^3 - (a + 3)|x|^2 + 1 & 0 \leq |x| \leq 1 \\ a|x|^3 - 5a|x|^2 + 8a|x| - 4a & 1 \leq |x| \leq 2 \\ 0 & 2 \leq |x| \end{cases}$$

The value a is used to control the shape of the kernel. Practical values for a are between -3 and 0. The closer a is to 0, the stronger the blurring effect you will get. The closer to -3 the value of a, the more sharpening you will see. In most cases, -0.5 is the best value to use.

Figure 5.16 shows the distance between the point to be interpolated and its four closest points. Knowing these distances simplifies the interpolation computations. As seen in Figure 5.4, interpolation consists of multiplying points by the values of an interpolation kernel at the points of intersection. Let's represent the kernel coefficients as c_0, c_1, c_2, and c_3. The points at x_0, x_1, x_2, and x_3 have values of p_0, p_1, p_2, and p_3. Our interpolated point is represented as

$$f(d) = c_0 \cdot p_0 + c_1 \cdot p_1 + c_2 \cdot p_2 + c_3 \cdot p_3$$

Knowing the equation for cubic convolution interpolation and the distances from our points to the interpolated points we can compute the kernel coefficients.

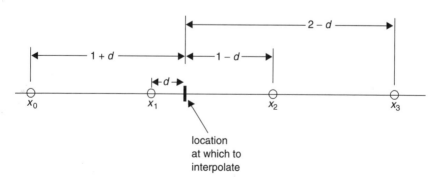

FIGURE 5.16 Distances from known points to interpolated point.

Plate 1.

Rendering of a dinosaur egg.
(Image courtesy of Jennifer Moyer, Hewlett-Packard Company.)

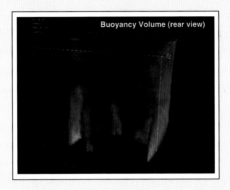

Buoyancy Volume (rear view)

Plate 2.

Single frame of a model of fire development.
(Image courtesy of the National Center for Atmospheric Research, Boulder, Colorado.)

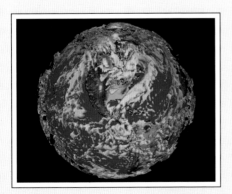

Plate 3.

Model of cloud development.
(Image courtesy of the National Center for Atmospheric Research, Boulder, Colorado.)

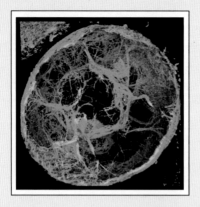

Plate 4.

Stage 1 frog ocyte rendered from more than 50 contiguous optical sections.
(Image courtesy of Vay Tek Inc.)

Plate 5.

Fetus.
(Photo courtesy of Vay Tek Inc.)

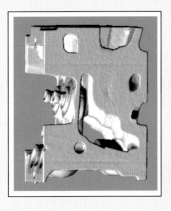

Plate 6.

Outer shell is rendered opaque.

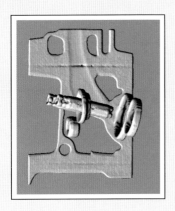

Plate 7.

The backplate and inner parts of the engine block consist of a different material.

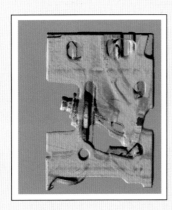

Plate 8.

Outer shell rendered partially transparent.

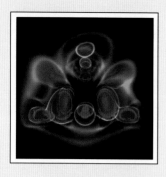

Plate 9.

Rendering of the high potential protein.
(Image courtesy of Hanspeter Pfister, Mitsubishi Electric Research Laboratory.)

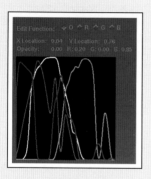

Plate 10.

Transfer functions used to generate rendering of high potential protein (Plate 4).
(Image courtesy of Hanspeter Pfister, Mitsubishi Electric Research Laboratory.)

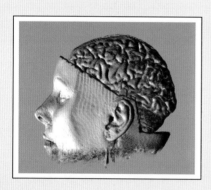

Plate 11.

Rendering without using segmentation information.

Plate 12.

Rendering using segmentation information and the same classification parameters as in Plate 6.

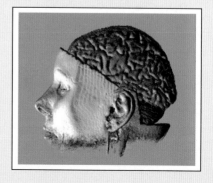

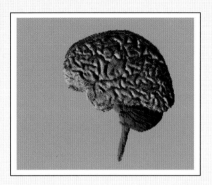

Plate 13.

Rendering using segmentation information. Skin and bone are made transparent in the classification stage.

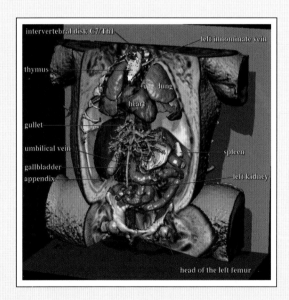

Plate 14.

Volume rendering of a torso. Organs are labeled and rendered in different colors.

(Image courtesy of the Institute of Math and Computer Science in Medicine, University of Hamburg.)

Plate 15.

Volume rendering of a lock. Using the opacity transfer function, the casing is made transparent. Different parts are labeled.

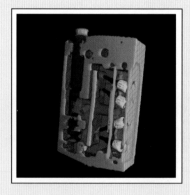

Plate 16.

Volume rendering of a lock. Using the RGB transfer function, the casing is made visible and colored blue.

Plate 17.

The self occlusion effect. Separate iterpolation of color and opacity.
(Data set courtesy of Ramani Pichumani, Stanford University School of Medicine. Image rendered by Tom Maltbender, Craig Wittenbrink, and Mike Goss.)

Plate 18.

The self occlusion effect. Opacity weighted interpolation of colors.
(Data set courtesy of Ramani Pichumani, Stanford University School of Medicine. Image rendered by Tom Maltbender, Craig Wittenbrink, and Mike Goss.)

Plate 19.

The self occlusion effect. Normalized difference image.
(Data set courtesy of Ramani Pichumani, Stanford University School of Medicine. Image rendered by Tom Maltbender, Craig Wittenbrink, and Mike Goss.)

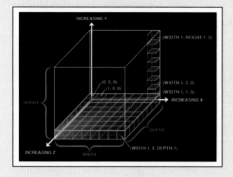

Plate 20.

Relationship of x, y, and z voxels within a volume.

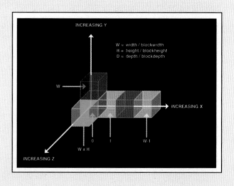

Plate 21.

Blocks of volume data within a larger volume.

$$c_0 = a(1 + d)^3 - 5a(1 + d)^2 + 8a(1 + d) - 4a$$
$$= ad^3 - 2ad^2 + ad$$

$$c_1 = (a + 2)d^3 - (a + 3)d^2 + 1$$
$$c_2 = (a + 2)(1 - d)^3 - (a + 3)(1 - d)^2 + 1$$
$$= (-1)(a + 2)d^3 + (2a + 3)d^2 - ad$$

$$c_3 = a(2 - d)^3 - 5a(2 - d)^2 + 8a(2 - d) - 4a$$
$$= -ad^3 + ad^2$$

As you can see, there are many computations just to compute the kernel coefficients. If you are implementing cubic convolution interpolation, you will want some type of optimization to speed up coefficient calculations. One speedup is to precalculate the coefficients and store them in a look-up table. If interested, see the For Further Study section. If you choose to compute the coefficients each time you interpolate, you will want to use Horner's rule. This is a simple recursive way of computing polynomials. We know that

$$x^2 + x = (x + 1)x$$

We can extend that further

$$x^3 + 2x^2 + 3x + 4 = (((x + 2)x + 3)x + 4)$$

The beauty of this simplification is that we have reduced a computation from five multiplications and three additions to two multiplications and three additions. These savings really add up, especially when interpolating millions of points per screen.

Just like linear interpolation, cubic convolution interpolation can easily be extended to two dimensions. This is shown in Figure 5.17. Since there are four points used in an interpolation, there are four interpolations to do in the x-direction. The resulting values are then interpolated in the y-direction. This method can be extended further to three dimensions.

Figure 5.18 shows the results of scaling our image by a factor of 4 and 15 via bicubic convolution interpolation. The results are very good.

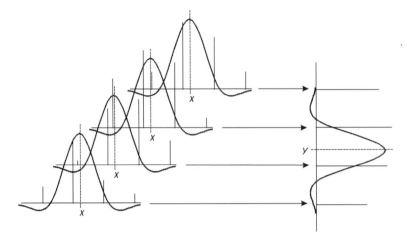

FIGURE 5.17   Extending cubic convolution interpolation to two dimensions.

a, b   **c**

FIGURE 5.18   (a) Original image; (b) scaled by a factor of 4 via bicubic convolution interpolation; (c) scaled by a factor of 15 via bicubic convolution interpolation.

B-Spline

The B-spline function is a purely positive, smoothing interpolation function. Splines are piecewise polynomials. The B-spline function is defined as

$$f(x) = \begin{cases} \frac{1}{2}|x|^3 - |x|^2 + \frac{2}{3} & 0 \le |x| < 1 \\ -\frac{1}{6}|x|^3 + |x|^2 - 2|x| + \frac{4}{3} & 1 \le |x| < 2 \\ 0 & 2 \le |x| \end{cases}$$

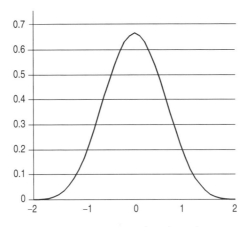

FIGURE 5.19   B-spline kernel.

The B-spline kernel is shown in Figure 5.19. It is a purely positive function and therefore requires no checking of the output for negative values. The ideal interpolation function is a low-pass filter and the B-spline function makes a pretty good low-pass filter.

The B-spline has a unique characteristic. All coefficients will add to 1.0. No matter where you place your four equidistant samples, the sum of the four coefficients will be 1. This allows for an optimization. Once the first three coefficients are computed, the fourth can be computed by subtracting the other three from 1.0. This saves some costly multiplies.

a, b    **c**

FIGURE 5.20   (a) Original image; (b) scaled by a factor of 4 via B-spline interpolation; (c) scaled by a factor of 15 via B-spline interpolation.

The results of scaling the original image using B-spline interpolation are shown in Figure 5.20. You can see the blurring effects of using the smooth B-spline function for interpolation.

VOLUME RENDERING EXAMPLE

In Figure 5.21 we show the difference between nearest neighbor and trilinear interpolation in volume rendering. These renderings are generated by oversampling with a factor of 2 in the z-direction, which means multiple samples per voxel are taken. In Figure 5.21(a) you can see a big hole in the front plate. Because of nearest neighbor sampling, the thin surface at the front is missed. Figure 5.21(b) shows much less aliasing. Using a different opacity transfer function will impact the result of the rendering. It is possible to find a transfer function that will almost completely cover the hole in Figure 5.21(a), for example. This means that, although linear interpolation exhibits considerably less aliasing, we should really consider the whole volume rendering pipeline when making statements about parameter trade-offs, like interpolation functions.

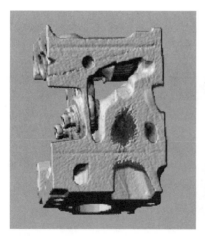
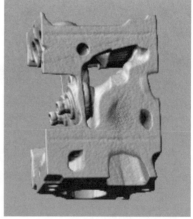

a   b

FIGURE 5.21   (a) Nearest neighbor interpolation; (b) linear interpolation.

TABLE 5.1 Number of Multiplications and Additions Necessary for Various Interpolation Methods on a One-Dimensional Signal

	Nearest Neighbor	Linear	Cubic Convolution	B-spline
Multiply	0	1	4	4
Add/Subtract	1	2	3	3

CONCLUSIONS

The quality of images interpolated using the various methods can be ranked as follows: bicubic convolution, B-spline, bilinear, and nearest neighbor. If image quality were your only concern, you would implement your volume renderer using tricubic convolution interpolation. Unfortunately, that method comes with a high price tag. Table 5.1 shows the number of multiplications and additions needed to execute the formulas in this chapter for a one-dimensional signal.

Although there doesn't seem to be a big difference between the number of computations, the differences explode as you extend into multiple dimensions. Table 5.2 shows the same computations in three dimensions.

A few notes concerning these numbers are in order. When using nearest neighbor interpolation, you need one addition per dimension for the rounding calculation. If you step along your ray using an integer address, no further rounding is necessary. Also the numbers shown for linear interpolation refer to the formula given. If you interpolate by sampling the interpolation kernel and multiplying the values at the intersections, the number of additions and mul-

TABLE 5.2 Number of Multiplications and Additions Necessary for Various Interpolation Methods on a Three-Dimensional Signal

	Nearest Neighbor	Linear	Cubic Convolution	B-spline
Multiply	0	7	52	52
Add/Subtract	3	14	39	39

tiplications should be swapped. These numbers do not include any optimizations discussed in this chapter. They also exclude all the costly computations necessary to generate the kernel coefficients for cubic convolution and B-spline interpolation. For this reason, you are discouraged from using these last two methods. If your application is not interactive, you can use tricubic convolution interpolation to give you the finest image quality possible. Numerous studies have concluded that cubic convolution interpolation often yields the best results. These studies have used such varying methods as image comparison, frequency response analysis, and comparison of error rates.

If your application is interactive, we would encourage you to consider trilinear interpolation. Trilinear interpolation reduces the aliasing problems seen when using nearest neighbor interpolation while keeping the number of computations per interpolation reasonable.

FOR FURTHER STUDY

There are many good papers on interpolation. Everyday more appear and many focus on optimizations of existing methods and analysis of the resulting image quality. If you wish to learn more about the interpolation functions presented in this chapter, we would suggest [145], [86], [116], and [187]. Also see Chapters 4, 5, and 6 of [257] which cover sampling theory, image resampling, and antialiasing.

For optimizations, you may want to start with [248]. It presents a method of storing interpolation coefficients in look-up tables for quick access.

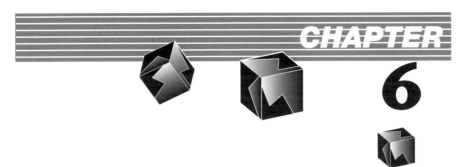

6

COMPOSITING

In Chapter 2 we discussed transformations and stepping along a ray. We also briefly introduced compositing, and we used one specific compositing operation, Maximum Intensity Projection, or MIP, as an example. In this chapter we will discuss the compositing operation in detail.

For each ray we cast through the data set, the stepping and interpolation stages generate a number of sample points on that ray. To determine the final pixel color, these sample points need to be combined. This process of combining is called compositing.

Compositing is in general a complex nonlinear operation. It is not intuitively easy to predict what the pixel color will be, given a set of sample points on a ray. Because of this it is also hard to understand what happens when the shading parameters are changed, or when the classification function is even slightly modified. We saw that in Chapters 3 and 4.

In the literature you will also encounter the term blending. Blending is used in the OpenGL context and defines how two RGBA (red, green, blue, alpha) values can be combined. As of version 1.1 of OpenGL, there are more than ten possible ways to combine two RGBA values. Some of those make sense for volume rendering; some of them do not. In this book we use the term com-

positing instead of blending, since the term compositing has historically been used in the volume rendering literature.

In this chapter we will first discuss the basis of volume rendering, the volume rendering integral. Here the shading, classification,
and compositing stages will be linked together. Then we will introduce the front-to-back and back-to-front methods of compositing.
We also show how to do this in software. Finally we will introduce
some other commonly used compositing operators.

THE RAY CASTING INTEGRAL

Let's go through some mathematical background with respect to ray
casting. If you are not interested in why ray casting works, or do not
want to see an integral ever, you can safely skip this section and the
next and go to the Front to Back Compositing section.

Ray casting produces an image by processing all the data
points in the volume data set. It assumes a certain behavior in
which the voxels in the data set scatter, occlude, generate, and reflect light. Several models have been proposed and analyzed. See
the For Further Study section for more information.

The ray casting algorithm in this book is based on the model
used by most ray casting applications today. The effects of light
shone upon a data set interacting with the sample along one viewing ray are typically integrated to form the final color of one pixel,
as follows:

$$I(a,b) = \int_a^b g(s)e^{-\int_a^s \tau(x)dx}ds \tag{6.1}$$

$I(a,b)$ is the intensity of one pixel. ds is the direction of the ray,
and the ray runs from a to b (see Figure 6.1). $g(s)$ is the source term.
It essentially describes the illumination model used in ray casting. It
can be a very simple direction-independent model or a sophisticated Phong model, as we discussed in Chapter 3. $\tau(x)$ is the extinction coefficient and defines the rate that light is occluded per unit
length due to scattering or extinction of light. This sounds rather
complicated, but $\tau(x)$ turns out to be nothing more than the transparency of one voxel. $g(s)$ and $\tau(x)$ are used to map a voxel value
into an intensity and opacity, respectively. We call them transfer

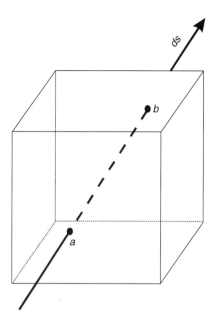

Figure 6.1 One ray through a volume. The ray enters the volume at point *a* and exits at point *b*. The direction of the ray is given as *ds*.

functions, as we saw in Chapter 4. They are the heart of the volume rendering algorithm.

The above formula describes a model that is based on real-world physical phenomena, namely the behavior of light when it hits a volume data set. Of course a computer cannot evaluate a continuous integral; thus for practical purposes this integral has to be approximated.

DISCRETIZATION OF THE RAY CASTING INTEGRAL

The simplest discrete approximation to a continuous integral is the Riemann sum. This approximation is widely used, and we are adopting it as well.

$$\int_0^d h(x)dx \approx \sum_{i=0}^{n} h(x_i)\Delta x \tag{6.2}$$

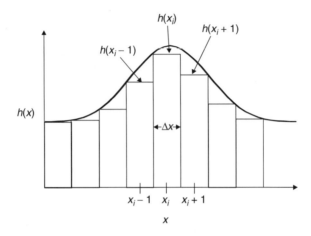

FIGURE 6.2   Discretization of a continuous function using a Riemann sum.

This equation describes how you can compute an integral if you have only a discrete set of samples from the original function $h(x)$ available. The interval between 0 and d is divided up into n equal intervals of length Δx. For each interval we assume the value of $h(x)$ to be constant, and that value is $h(x_i)$. Figure 6.2 shows the continuous function $h(x)$ divided up into small intervals with a constant value.

Now suppose we have already computed the intensity and transparency on one ray at discrete sample points. The discrete front-to-back version of the ray integral then becomes

$$I(a,b) = \sum_{i=0}^{n} I_i \prod_{j=0}^{i-1} T_j \qquad (6.3)$$

I_i is the total light emitted, or intensity, of a point at position i on the ray, and T_j is the transparency of one point on the ray. Transparency is a number between zero and one. It represents how much light goes through a point. Figure 6.3 shows one ray through a data set, and the sample points on that ray. Equation (6.3) will have to be evaluated for all rays cast through the data set.

Quite often you will see opacity mentioned instead of transparency. The opacity is defined as one minus the transparency:

$$\alpha = 1 - T \qquad (6.4)$$

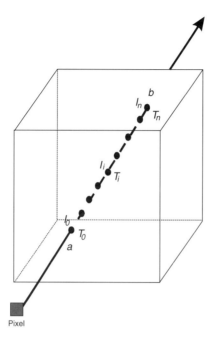

FIGURE 6.3   There are nine sample points on one ray ($n = 8$). Each sample point has an intensity and a transparency.

Later on we will see why it is computationally more efficient to use transparencies than opacities.

FRONT-TO-BACK COMPOSITING

If we use opacity instead of transparency in Equation (6.3) we get the often-used front-to-back ray casting formula:

$$I(a,b) = \sum_{i=0}^{n} I_i \prod_{j=0}^{i-1}(1 - \alpha_j) \qquad (6.5)$$

Intuitively Equation (6.5) tells us that the total intensity I accumulated on one ray at the current sample point is the intensity I_i multiplied with all the transparencies, $(1 - \alpha_j)$ encountered so far on the ray. Thus I_i is weighted by all preceding sample points. Figure 6.4 shows a front-to-back example on one ray. Sample points

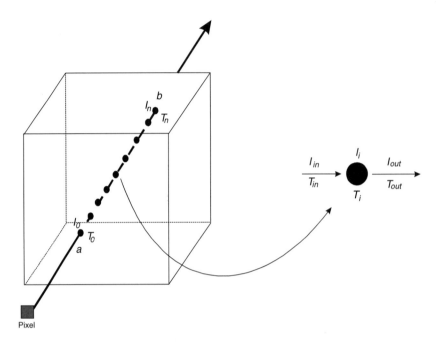

Pixel

FIGURE 6.4 Front-to-back compositing. Sample points are composited together in a front-to-back way, starting at point *a* and working toward point *b* on the ray. The closeup shows the situation at one sample point.

are composited starting at point *a* on the ray and working toward the exiting point *b*. On the right we show the situation for one sample point. The intensity I_{in} and transparency T_{in} are the composited values up to this sample point. Front-to-back compositing I_i and T_i with I_{in} and T_{in} results in the new values I_{out} and T_{out}. There is also a back-to-front compositing equation.

Note that the intensity I_i is not the same as the color of a sample point. In the literature you will almost always find the following relationship between intensity and color:

$$I_i = C_i * \alpha_i \tag{6.6}$$

Thus the intensity is the color of the sample point multiplied with the opacity of that sample point. However, this is certainly not the only possible way to define intensity. In the For Further Study section, there are references to papers that discuss this in more detail. In this book we will use the above definition, since it is the most common one.

In order to compute $I(a,b)$ we need to recursively evaluate the ray casting formula. This can be seen quite easily by writing out Equation (6.5):

$$\sum_{i=0}^{n} I_i \prod_{j=0}^{i-1}(1 - \alpha_j) = I_0 + I_1(1 - \alpha_0)$$

$$+ I_2(1 - \alpha_0)(1 - \alpha_1) + ... + I_n(1 - \alpha_0) ... (1 - \alpha_{n-1}) \quad (6.7)$$

$$= I_0 \, over \, I_1 \, over \, I_2 \, over \, ... \, over \, I_n$$

Here we introduce the *over* operator. This operator was first introduced by Porter and Duff for digital imaging in their 1984 SIG-GRAPH paper. Thus compositing means applying the over operator on all sample points on one ray. Another way of writing the recursion algorithmically is given below. (Refer to Figure 6.4.)

$$I_{out} = I_{in} + T_{in}I_i$$
$$T_{out} = T_{in}T_i \quad\quad\quad\quad (6.8)$$

I_{out} and T_{out} are the total accumulated intensity and transparency just after the ray hit the current sample point. I_{in} and T_{in} are the total accumulated intensity and transparency just before the ray hit the sample point. I_i and T_i are the intensity and transparency of the current sample point. The following code can be used in a computer program to implement the front-to-back ray casting formula. First we will need to set the start conditions:

```
Trans = 1.0;
Inten = I[0];
```

Now we need to apply the following two equations for all sample points on a ray:

```
for (i = 1; i <= n; i++)
{
        Trans = Trans * T[i-1];
        Inten = Inten + Trans * I[i];
}
```

As you can see, we need to keep track of the accumulated transparency separately. This is good and bad. It is bad because it will take more time to render. The processor has to evaluate the transparency equation for every sample point. It is good because a smart software program can stop processing the current ray when Trans is zero or very close to zero. Any sample point composited after Trans reaches zero will not contribute anything anymore. Trans will stay zero. Thus it is useless to process the current ray any further. This is called early ray termination. Depending on the opacity transfer function, early ray termination can buy you a lot. If the transfer function is relatively sharp, there is a very good chance a ray will hit an opaque voxel early on in the data set and you can stop processing the current ray. You can expect to see a factor of two or more speedup compared to doing no early ray termination at all.

BACK-TO-FRONT COMPOSITING

So far we have talked about the front-to-back ray casting formula. There is a counterpart too, and it is not surprisingly called the back-to-front formula (see also Figure 6.5). As you can see in this figure the image plane did not move compared to Figure 6.4. The only difference is the order in which the sample points are processed. I_{out} and T_{out} are the total accumulated intensity and transparency just after the ray hits the current sample point. I_{in} and T_{in} are the total accumulated intensity and transparency just before the ray hit the sample point. I_i and T_i are the intensity and transparency of the current sample point. The back-to-front compositing equation is

$$I(a,b) = \sum_{i=0}^{n} I_i \prod_{j=i+1}^{n} (1 - \alpha_j) \qquad (6.9)$$

Or written recursively

$$I_{out} = I_{in}T_i + I_i \qquad (6.10)$$

This formula is almost identical to the front-to-back one, and it probably is not surprising to learn that they both generate the exact same results. It does not matter if you work your way from front to back, or back to front, through the data set. Then what is the differ-

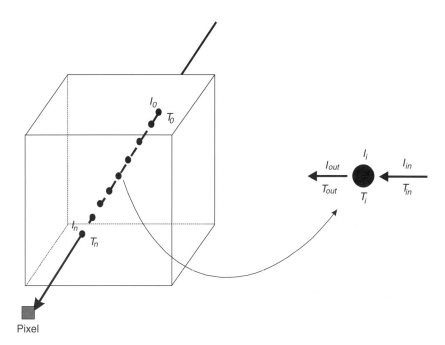

FIGURE 6.5 Back-to-front compositing. Sample points are composited together in a back-to-front way, starting at the back of the data set working toward the front of the ray. The zoomup shows the situation at one sample point.

ence? It has to do with the actual implementation. The following code will clarify that. First we will need to set the start condition:

```
Inten = I[0];
```

Now we need to apply the following equation for all sample points on the ray:

```
for (i = 1; i <= n; i++)
        Inten = Inten * T[i] + I[i];
```

As you can see we do not need to keep track of the accumulated transparency anymore. That means that the processor has less work to do per sample point compared to the front-to-back formula. However, it also means that early ray termination is no longer possible.

USING OPACITY INSTEAD OF TRANSPARENCY

In 1988, Levoy published one of the most-often cited papers in volume rendering. Instead of using transparency in his equations, he used opacity. Levoy also assumes the same relationship as in Equation (6.6) between intensity and color. What is important here is that the intensities in Equations (6.5, 6.7, 6.8, 6.9, and 6.10) have to be replaced by the color of a sample point multiplied by its opacity. As we have already said, opacity is the same as one minus the transparency. The reason we used transparency in the previous section is that it is slightly more computationally efficient than using opacities. If we write the front-to-back formula using opacities and substitute $I = C * \alpha$ we will get this:

$$C_{out} = C_{in} + (1 - \alpha_{in})\alpha_i C_i$$
$$\alpha_{out} = \alpha_{in} + \alpha_i(1 - \alpha_{in}) \tag{6.11}$$

As you can see there is one more subtraction to compute C_{out}, compared to I_{out} in Equation (6.8). To compute α_{out} we need to do one more addition and one more subtraction, compared to computing T_{out} in Equation (6.8). Thus, it is faster from a computing standpoint of view to use transparencies instead of opacities. In the literature, however, you will see Equation (6.11) used almost exclusively.

The following code can be used to compute an image using front-to-back compositing and opacities:

```
alpha = 0.0;
Inten = 0.0;
```

Now we need to apply the following two equations for all sample points on a ray.

```
for (i = 0; i <= n; i++)
{
        Inten = Inten + (1 - alpha) * I[i] * A[i];
        alpha = alpha + A[i] * (1 - alpha);
}
```

To generate color images you will need to do this for each color channel, once for red, green, and blue. Of course you first will have to set a color transfer function that converts voxel intensities into colors.

If you want another background than black behind the volume you are rendering, simply repeat the compositing one more time with the desired color of the background. Thus,

```
Inten = Inten + (1 - alpha) * Background;
```

Since the background is the very last sample on the ray, you do not need to update α_{out} anymore. We also assumed that the background is completely opaque; thus $\alpha_{background} = 1.0$.

Levoy reported only the back-to-front formula in his 1988 paper. It is

$$C_{out} = C_i\alpha_i + C_{in}(1 - \alpha_i)$$

Again, we do not need to keep track of the accumulated opacities in the back-to-front compositing mode. The following code can be used to compute an image using back-to-front compositing and opacities:

```
Inten = 0.0;
```

Now we need to apply the following equation to all sample points on the ray:

```
for (i = 0; i <= n; i++)
            Inten = I[i] * A[i] + Inten * (1 - A[i]);
```

If you want a colored background, set the start intensity to the background color you want.

PARTIAL RAY COMPOSITING

Ray casting is a compute-intensive operation, and it can take a long time to render one frame even on a state-of-the-art computer. Of course this depends on the data set size. For data sets that are common these days, compute power definitely is the limiting factor. This is the reason that many publications discuss ways to parallelize ray casting. One very important and nice property of the front-to-back or the back-to-front compositing mode is partial ray compositing. This means that you can chop a ray in two (or more) parts at any point on the ray and treat them as two completely different rays. After you composite each of these two new rays, which results in two colors, you will only need to combine these two colors using the over operator to get the final pixel color. What is the advantage of doing this? It allows you to divide a data set up into smaller chunks and have a multiprocessor computer, or a distributed set of computers on a network, work on the chunks in parallel (see Figure 6.6). Here we divided the data set into two chunks. Each processor can work on its own chunk independently from the other processor. Each processor generates an image for the part of the data set it is working on. Once both images are rendered, the two images are composited using the over operator, resulting in the final image.

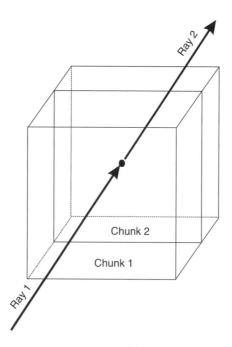

FIGURE 6.6 Partial ray compositing. It is possible to work on ray 1 and ray 2 in parallel, composite the values on each of the partial rays, and then composite the two results.

OPACITY CORRECTION WHEN OVERSAMPLING

We are free to choose the number of sample points on one ray, as long as we stay above the Nyquist sampling frequency to avoid aliasing. However, the result of the compositing operating should be independent of the number of sample points on one ray. If we take more sample points, we will composite more opacity values, which will result in a final composited opacity value that is higher. Unless we correct for this, the translucency of a rendered object depends on the number of sample points. Since compositing is a non-linear operation, simply dividing by the total number of sample points on one ray does not solve this.

Let us assume a homogeneous data set with constant opacity α_m everywhere and the same color C_m throughout. If we take only one sample point on a ray through this material we get, using back-to-front compositing

$$C_{out} = C_{in}(1 - \alpha_m) + C_m\alpha_m \tag{6.12}$$

Now, if we take N sample points through the same data set, we get

$$C_{out} = \sum_{i=0}^{N} I_i \prod_{j=i+1}^{N} (1 - \alpha_j)$$

Since we assumed the material to be homogenous, all opacities are the same, $\alpha_j = \alpha$. Using this and substitution $I_i = C_i\alpha_i$ we get

$$C_{out} = C_{in}\prod_{j=1}^{N}(1 - \alpha) + \sum_{i=1}^{N} C_m\alpha \prod_{j=i+1}^{N} (1 - \alpha) \tag{6.13}$$

Here we factored the first term out, for $i = 0$. Equation (6.12) and Equation (6.13) have to yield the same result. This means that

$$C_{in}(1 - \alpha_m) = C_{in}\prod_{j=1}^{N}(1 - \alpha)$$

Since the material is homogeneous, the opacity values are constant, independent of j:

$$(1 - \alpha_m) = (1 - \alpha)^N$$

Opacity values are always between zero and one. Therefore we can rewrite this to

$$\alpha = 1 - \sqrt[N]{1 - \alpha_m} \qquad (6.14)$$

Thus when oversampling, that is, taking samples with a distance less than the unit distance apart, each acquired opacity will have to be rescaled according to Equation (6.14). Given the oversampling factor N, Equation (6.14) can be precomputed and stored in a look-up table.

OPACITY WEIGHTED COLOR INTERPOLATION

There are two popular configurations of the volume rendering pipeline. The first one classifies and shades voxels and then interpolates the resulting RGBA values down to the sample points on a ray. The other flavor interpolates the gradients and voxel intensity values down to the sample points and then performs the classification and shading on the sample point. Discussion of the merits for each flavor is not the topic of this section. We will focus on the former method where classification and shading are done at the voxel locations.

When interpolating colors and opacities down to the sample point on a ray, it is important to weigh the colors with their respective opacities first, before doing the interpolation. Opacity weighted colors are also called *associated colors* in the literature. This means that we need to interpolate the opacities and the associated colors down to the sample point and then blend the result of those interpolations.

Given a neighborhood of eight voxels each with a color C_v and opacity α_v, $v = 1.8$, we need to interpolate the opacities and associated colors as follows:

$$\alpha_{sample} = \sum_{v=1}^{8} w_v \alpha_v$$

where w_v are the interpolation weights.

$$C_{sample} = \sum_{v=1}^{8} w_v \alpha_v C_v$$

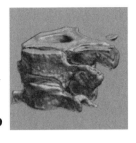

a, b   **c**

FIGURE 6.7 The self occlusion effect: (a) Separate interpolation of color and opacity; (b) opacity weighted interpolation of colors; (c) normalized difference image. (Data set courtesy of Ramani Pichumani, Stanford University School of Medicine. Images rendered by Tom Malzbender, Craig Wittenbrink, and Mike Goss, Hewlett-Packard Laboratories.)

Now we can do the blending using α_{sample} and C_{sample}. If we do not weigh the colors with their respective opacities, but instead interpolate only the colors, $C_{sample} = \Sigma_{v=1}^{8} w_v C_v$, we get the *self-occlusion* effect. See the For Further Study section for more information. Figure 6.7(a) and Plate 17 shows a volume rendering of a human vertebrae, not using associated colors. In this data set voxels in empty space ($\alpha = 0$) have been classified so that they are assigned the color red. Figure 6.7(b) and Plate 18 shows a volume rendering of the same data from the same viewpoint, but now with associated colors. Figure 6.7(c) and Plate 19 shows a normalized difference image. You can clearly see that the voxels with color red, but opacity of zero, do contribute to the rendering, whereas they should not.

OTHER COMPOSITING OPERATIONS

Front-to-back and back-to-front compositing are probably the two most important compositing operations. There are many more, however, that have proven to be valuable. Two of those will be discussed in this section.

Maximum Intensity Projection

We first saw the maximum intensity projection in Chapter 2. Maximum Intensity Projection, or MIP, is conceptually very simple. For each ray that goes through the data set, find the maximum intensity value on that ray. This value is the final pixel value. Thus MIP will visualize bright structures in a data set. MIP is traditionally used in medical imaging. MRA (Magnetic Resonance Angiography) techniques produce a data set where the voxels that are part of blood vessels have very bright intensity values. MIP is the perfect technique to visualize those blood vessels. Doctors can use MIP to estimate if an artery is partially blocked and decide if surgery is necessary or not. Figure 6.8 shows an MIP rendering of a Magnetic Resonance (MR) data set of a human head.

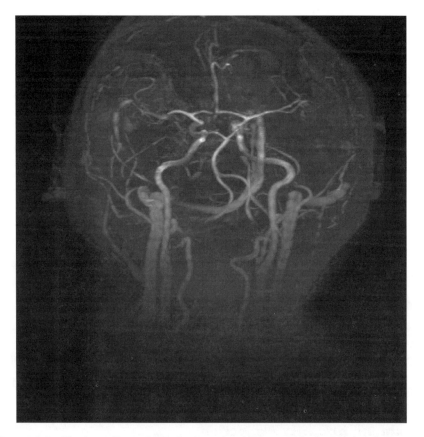

FIGURE 6.8   Maximum Intensity Projection of an MRI scan of a human head. (Data set courtesy of Allen Anderson, Medical Imaging Research Laboratory, Department of Radiology, University of Utah.)

X-ray Projection

This compositing mode will generate images that are very similar to conventional X-rays that are taken in a hospital. Instead of compositing sample values on a ray using the over operator, we add all the intensity values on one ray. The result is the displayed pixel value. This compositing mode is also called SUM, for obvious reasons. If you are implementing this, you should be careful not to overflow the variable you are using to store the sum. You might have to normalize the sum after a ray is completed so as not to exceed the dynamic range of your video card. See Figure 6.9 for an example of an X-ray projection of the engine block. We have used this same data set for renderings in previous chapters.

Another way of achieving the same result, but in a fundamentally faster way, is using so-called Fourier volume rendering. This method uses fast Fourier techniques to extract the frequency spectrum of the projection of the data set in the Fourier domain and computes the projection by applying an inverse two-dimensional

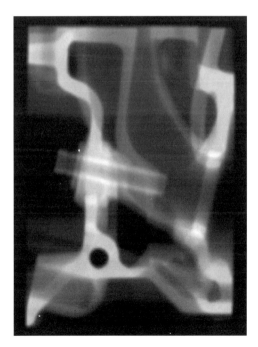

FIGURE 6.9 X-ray (SUM) projection of engine block.

Fourier transformation to that spectrum. Since the computational complexity is reduced from three dimensions to two dimensions, this can be a very attractive method to use when generating X-ray-like images.

FOR FURTHER STUDY

Volume rendering is based on the physics of light interaction with particles in a volume. Early work in this field is described in [15] and extended in [117].

Compositing originally was described in [15] and [181]. Volume rendering algorithms described in [43], [129], [206], and [240] are all based on those compositing ideas. These four papers were all printed in the same SIGGRAPH '88 proceedings, another good resource to have. In [148] you will find an excellent analysis of the volume rendering integral. [16] describes compositing in a very readable way.

The self-occlusion effect blends in colors even if these colors are totally transparent. Therefore there is some contribution to the final pixel color. Multiplying the color with its opacity will guarantee that there is no contribution, if the opacity is zero. This effect is analyzed in [164]. Unfortunately the volume rendering pipeline discussed in [129], [131], and [133] erroneously interpolates color values independent of their opacities.

The [129] paper, [253] course, [10] and [170] theses are more practically oriented. They apply compositing in volume rendering. In [10] you will find proof that the back-to-front and front-to-back compositing equations do yield exactly the same result.

Fourier volume rendering was originally published in [146] and [47]. Since all processing is done in the Fourier domain, and since the Fourier transformation is a linear operation, nonlinear effects like lighting and shading are hard to incorporate. In [232] an attempt was made to add (linear) shading effects.

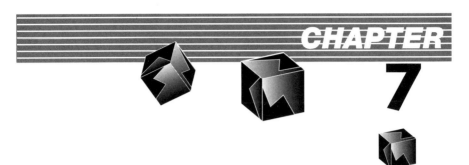

VOLUME SLICING

Volume visualization does not always require the type of volume rendering pipeline that has been presented thus far. Before direct volume rendering techniques were developed and before current computational capabilities, discrete three-dimensional volume data sets could be visualized as a single two-dimensional image slice, one slice at a time. These slices could be orthogonal slices aligned with the volume data voxels, they could be orthogonal slices located between volume data voxels, or they could be slices oblique to the original volume data set. The technique of resampling a two-dimensional image slice from a three-dimensional volume data set is known as multiplanar reformatting. Multiplanar reformatting is used in medical applications to *scan* an image from a data set that has already been collected. In seismic applications, multiplanar reformatting provides a method to generate arbitrary cross sections from a large and opaque data set. Figure 7.1 shows an oblique multiplanar reformatted image of a volume data set.

The volume rendering framework described in Chapter 2 introduced the concept of ray casting through a volume. As each ray was cast through the volume, samples were taken at regular intervals and were eventually composited into a single value that was used to color the pixel on the projection plane associated with the ray. Multiplanar reformatting locates the projection plane within the

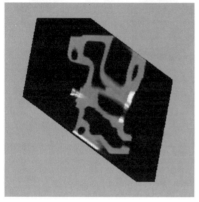 

a   b

FIGURE 7.1 (a) Multiplanar reformatted rendering; (b) maximum intensity projection rendering from the same view.

volume. Samples are taken where the projection plane pixels are located within the volume data set. Figure 7.2 shows the relationship of the projection plane with the volume data set. The line represents the projection plane through the data set. The values of the pixels on the projection plane are acquired by resampling the voxels around a pixel. Typically this is done using trilinear interpolation to avoid aliasing artifacts.

Volume transformation was explained in Chapter 2. The benefit of inverse transformations for ray casting was discussed in depth. For multiplanar reformatting, we will again use the inverse transformation to implement the renderer.

Equation (7.1), the transformation matrix, describes the orientation of a volume with respect to a projection plane. The inverse of the transformation matrix, shown in Equation (7.2), will describe how the projection plane maps onto the original volume in volume coordinate space. This is exactly the same transformation that generated samples along a ray for the volume rendering framework.

$$
\begin{bmatrix}
a & e & i & m \\
b & f & j & n \\
c & g & k & o \\
0 & 0 & 0 & 1
\end{bmatrix}
$$

EQUATION 7.1 Transformation matrix.

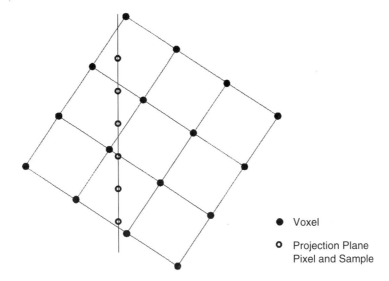

FIGURE 7.2   Multiplanar reformatting conceptual diagram.

$$\begin{bmatrix} al & el & il & ml \\ bl & fl & jl & nl \\ cl & gl & kl & ol \\ 0 & 0 & 0 & 1 \end{bmatrix} = inverse \left(\begin{bmatrix} a & e & i & m \\ b & f & j & n \\ c & g & k & o \\ 0 & 0 & 0 & 1 \end{bmatrix} \right)$$

EQUATION 7.2   Inverse transformation matrix.

Multiplanar reformatting does not require samples along a ray. Instead, only a single sample is required, in essence, only the first sample of the ray. Calculation of this sample point is shown in Equation (7.3) where the projection plane pixel represented by the $(x, y, 0)$ point is transformed using the inverse transformation matrix to a real sample point (x', y', z') located within the volume data set.

$$\begin{bmatrix} al & el & il & ml \\ bl & fl & jl & nl \\ cl & gl & kl & ol \\ 0 & 0 & 0 & 1 \end{bmatrix} \times \begin{bmatrix} x \\ y \\ 0 \\ 1 \end{bmatrix} = \begin{bmatrix} x' \\ y' \\ z' \\ 1 \end{bmatrix}$$

EQUATION 7.3   Transforming a projection plane pixel.

As with ray casting, the real sample point (x', y', z') requires interpolation within the neighborhood as explained in Chapters 2 and 5.

Since multiplanar reformatting consists of a single sample per projection plane pixel, it results in fewer interpolated points than when casting rays. More sophisticated three-dimensional interpolation techniques such as trilinear or tricubic can be employed, while still achieving reasonable computing times.

Transformations along a ray can be optimized. Transform the first sample point and then "step" to the next sample point by incrementing the current sample point by the z-vector portion of the inverse transformation matrix. A similar optimization can be used for multiplanar reformatting. After determining the first sample point for a pixel in a row within the projection plane, the next sample point along the row can be determined by simply incrementing the sample point by the x-vector portion of the inverse transformation matrix.

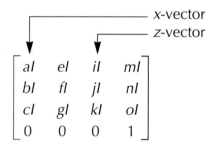

EQUATION 7.4 x- and z-vectors within an inverse transformation matrix.

For applications where experts interact with regions of volume data sets that are very familiar, multiplanar reformatting can be a very effective visualization tool. Experts in the medical and seismic fields are often trained to reconstruct complex structures in their minds while actually viewing only slices of the three-dimensional volume data set.

FOR FURTHER STUDY

To learn more about multiplanar reformatting and its applications, see Reference 273.

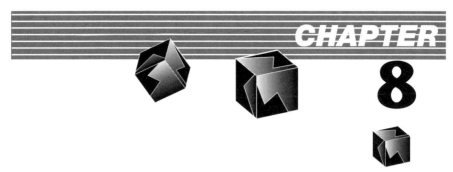

CHAPTER

8

TRADE-OFFS

Volume rendering is a resource demanding process. Continual advancements in computer technology tempt us into thinking interactive volume rendering will be available soon. Computational power is quickly usurped by greedy volume rendering applications that want more functionality and more quality and also by ever-growing data sets. For this reason, the pursuit of better volume rendering architectures, algorithms, and compromises are always warranted. Let us examine some of the performance issues and potential solutions that accompany our search for the elusive *real-time* volume renderer.

A HIGH-PERFORMANCE VOLUME VISUALIZATION SYSTEM

Volume rendering taxes every component of a computer system. Whether we are considering a software implementation of a volume renderer or a hardware solution, we encounter limitations and bottlenecks in all computer system components. The compute-intensive nature of volume rendering can subdue even the fastest desktop computer available today. A volume rendering pipeline, as in Figure 8.1, consisting of gradient calculation, classification, shad-

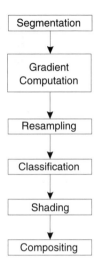

FIGURE 8.1   The volume rendering pipeline.

ing, resampling, and compositing is a formidable series of computations as we have shown.

Furthermore, since we must pass a sizable volume through the volume rendering process for a single rendering, performance can often be a illusion at best. If we could create some specialized acceleration hardware that could perform this set of calculations quickly, we would then be in business. Well, specialized hardware may speed up the computations, but we encounter a few problems.

Computer System Resources and Bottlenecks

Figure 8.2 shows a typical computer system block diagram employing a volume rendering accelerator. Because volumes reside in physical memory on a computer system, we must read the volume from memory and pass it to our hardware accelerator, across several data buses.

Memory accesses are pretty quick these days and some very fast memory and peripheral buses provide us a pretty fast I/O path. However, the issue of how our hardware accelerator performs its calculations needs to be addressed. Since we created an auxiliary processor to do our calculations, it must access the volume data set. In order to traverse the complete volume, our accelerator needs to

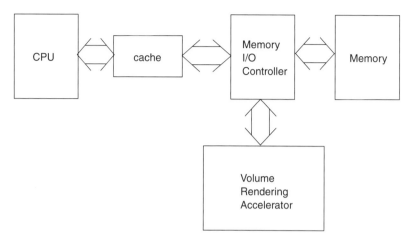

FIGURE 8.2 Computer system block diagram.

have access to that data in memory. We could just pass the whole volume to our volume accelerator, but then the accelerator will need to be equipped with its own (sizable) memory and we will have the wasteful situation of maintaining two copies of our volume. This also limits the size of volumes that can be rendered to the amount of memory equipped on our accelerator. To avoid this costly architecture, we need to provide our hardware accelerator with the parts of the volume it needs, when it needs it. The volume can be transferred from memory to the accelerator either through Direct Memory Access (DMA) or Programmed I/O (PIO). DMA has the advantage that data can be moved without extensive involvement of the main processor. However, DMA requires some significant volume storage on the part of the volume accelerator. Programmed I/O can move more manageable pieces of the volume to the volume accelerator but requires the resources of the main processor and its memory cache.

If you recall the algorithms that we formulated in building our volume renderer, you will remember that gradient calculations and resampling require access to neighborhoods of voxels in the x-, y-, and z-dimensions. This situation unfortunately causes another problem. For volumes stored in memory such that neighboring voxels along the x-axis are adjacent, neighboring voxels along the y-axis are one row of x-axis voxels apart. The locality of neighboring voxels along the *z*-axis is even worse. They are one row of *x*-axis voxels times one column of *y*-axis voxels apart. This volume storage relationship is shown in Figure 8.3 and Plate 20.

We mentioned that memory reads are pretty quick these days and memory buses are quite fast. However, the truth is that they really aren't fast enough; CPUs are designed to make use of caching to optimize memory accesses. Caching maintains copies of sequential memory registers of a defined size (cache line) in memory that can be accessed by the CPU very quickly . Because of the voxel organization shown in Figure 8.3, it is clear that our volume data sets are somewhat incompatible with cache optimization. Although some graphics accelerators are optimized for three-dimensional data access, CPU caches are not, which renders caching almost useless when volume rendering.

However, we can solve this by reorganizing our volume data in system memory. What is really needed is to fit a complete vol-

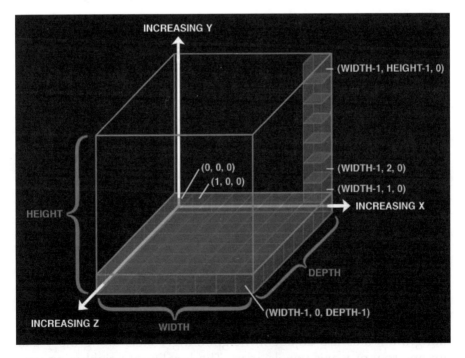

FIGURE 8.3 Relationship of *x*, *y*, and *z* voxels within a volume.

ume into a cache line. Perhaps not a complete volume, maybe just a small portion of our volume; a volume-in-a-volume. Let's call this small volume a block. Blocks can be processed very quickly.

Data Organization

Blocking is a natural quantization for volume data. Volumes can be broken into regular, gridded blocks encompassing a portion of a subdivided volume. This makes rendering of the block more manageable. A $16 \times 16 \times 16$ block of voxels consists of 4K voxels. For 2-byte voxels, a block consumes only 8K of memory. An 8K chunk of data easily fits within a cache of typical CPUs available today. This size is also a manageable local memory size required for a hardware accelerator. Figure 8.4 and Plate 21 shows the relationship of multiple blocks within a volume data set.

Since the volume rendering pipeline requires a neighborhood of voxels to properly perform gradient calculations and interpolations, a block needs to be "self-contained." To satisfy this require-

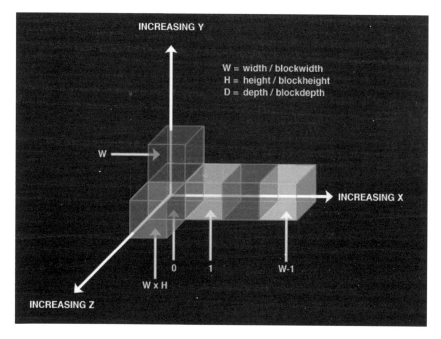

FIGURE 8.4 Blocks of volume data within a larger volume.

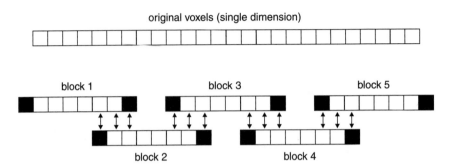

FIGURE 8.5 Voxels in a block need to overlap for resampling and gradient computation.

ment, border voxels and their adjacent neighbor voxels need to be included in a volume block. Volume blocks need to be doubly overlapped. Bordering voxels need to exist in all blocks that border that voxel. The next adjacent voxel is required for gradient computation. Figure 8.5 shows the overlapping required to establish completely self-contained blocks.

Overlapping blocks can be avoided in an architecture if the hardware accelerator or CPU is able to cache all neighboring blocks. This architecture will sustain the overhead of transmitting some blocks multiple times. Nevertheless, it is an architectural trade-off for appropriate implementations.

A block architecture improves feeding a volume accelerator for both DMA (Direct Memory Access) and PIO (Programmed Input/Output) I/O methods. Blocks are especially valuable for use with DMA. Ideal block sizes that maximize the throughput with respect to the I/O bandwidth, the volume accelerator cache, and processing speed can be determined.

Compression

Volumes are regional by nature. Neighboring voxels tend to be similar, especially where data does not contain anything of interest. An example of this is the sample locations outside of the body in medical data. The constant frequency nature of these regions provides opportunity to compress the data within the block quite well. Compression methods as simple as run-length encoding can be used. If more complex frequency based methods are desired, they are more easily implemented when volumes are organized in blocks. Compressed blocks can be decompressed on-the-fly by our hardware accelerator. Employing compression techniques saves memory resources and increases the effective I/O bandwidths of a volume rendering accelerator.

Pipelining

A volume rendering process is composed of many stages where voxels contribute to gradient calculation and classification, are shaded, transformed, interpolated, and composited. Voxels travel through the rendering pipeline and are subjected to these operations. Each stage can take a different amount of time to execute. We can conceive of a voxel traveling through the rendering pipeline where only a single voxel can occupy the pipeline at a time.

In a software implementation, this is conceptually what happens during rendering since a single processor can perform only one operation on one voxel at a time. For architectures that offer multiple CPUs or better yet, specialized volume rendering hardware that can perform specialized operations, performance opportunities arise. We must reevaluate how voxels flow through the pipeline. If multiple stages can operate on voxels simultaneously, a volume can be processed in less time than if only one operation could be performed at a time. This optimization is called pipelining. If each volume rendering stage took the same amount of time, the pipelined operations would be utilized with 100 percent efficiency (see Figure 8.6). However, other than for very simple and redundant operations, this is almost never the case. Pipelining alone is not enough to design a complex hardware or multiprocessing volume renderer. We also need to consider the aspects of parallel architectures.

Parallel Architectures

When more than one processor or hardware component performs different volume rendering operations at one time, the pipeline can be fed as fast as the slowest operation can be performed; the slowest operation is considered the *bottleneck*. The pipeline can be sped up by duplicating the slowest operator within the pipeline. Parallelization moves the bottleneck to the next slowest operation (see Figure 8.7).

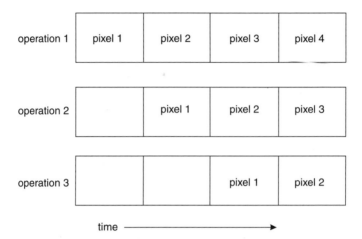

FIGURE 8.6   Fully pipelined processing sequences.

Pipe 1

operation 1	pixel 1	pixel 2	pixel 3	pixel 4
operation 2		pixel 1	pixel 2	pixel 3
operation 3			pixel 1	pixel 2

Pipe 2

operation 1	pixel 1	pixel 2	pixel 3	pixel 4
operation 2		pixel 1	pixel 2	pixel 3
operation 3			pixel 1	pixel 2

time ——————————————————————▶

FIGURE 8.7   Parallel pipelines.

Complete volume rendering pipelines can be used in parallel. When multiple pipelines render a single volume, we need to consider how we will feed the pipelines. Assuming each volume rendering pipeline performs ray casting and the volume data set is organized as a whole, each pipeline can be assigned half the volume to render or each pipeline can be assigned half the rays to cast. The former is considered object-space parallelism while the latter is considered image-space parallelism. Thanks to the concept of partial ray compositing, discussed in Chapter 6, this technique will work.

Precision

When implementing these algorithms in software, the precision issues are straightforward. If you need more precision in C, use the **double** keyword instead of **float**. When dealing with hardware acceleration, precision is not as easy to adjust.

Hardware stores non-integers as two types of numbers: floating point and fixed point. Floating point represents numbers in scientific notation and is used in CPUs and embedded controllers. Dedicated hardware accelerators often use fixed-point representation. Fixed-point representation allocates a number of bits to represent the integer portion of the number and another number of bits to represent the fractional portion of the number. When allocating the number of bits to represent your number, keep in mind how many operations will be executed. Sometimes this is easy to overlook.

During the compositing operation, a huge number of accumulations are performed. You do not want to ignore components of the accumulation simply because they appear too small. When a large number of small values are accumulated, they sum to an appreciable value. Ignore this fact and prepare to spend many nights trying to account for your crude renderings.

You must also increase your word length during accumulations if accuracy is not to be lost by underflow or overflow. The rule of thumb is:

For N additions, allow $\log 2N$ extra bits to guarantee no overflow in your accumulation.

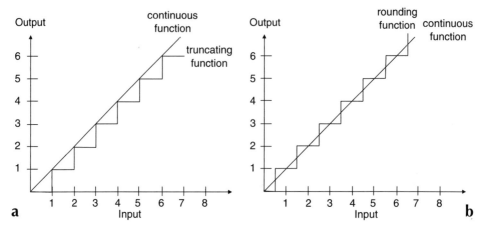

FIGURE 8.8   (a) Truncating a continuous function; (b) rounding a continuous function.

Multiplication is pretty straightforward. The rule of thumb is:

The product of two b-bit unsigned numbers requires $2b$ bits.

The results of hardware arithmetic often have higher precision than the final result for that datum. Examples of reduced final precision include pixels in a frame buffer or transferred over an I/O data bus. When reducing precision of a final value, rounding is highly preferred over truncation. Rounding is easily done with an addition followed by a truncation operation. For example to round the value 1.6 to the next integer, add 0.5 (to yield 2.1) and then drop the fractional value to get 2. Figure 8.8 shows the advantage of representing your final value with a rounding operation over the simple truncation. It is clear that rounding is a much closer approximation to the continuous function than simple truncation.

IMAGE QUALITY IMPROVEMENTS

Volume rendering is a compute-intensive operation, as you know by now. There are several trade-offs you can make to improve the rendering speed while giving up some image quality. This section will discuss some options you have to do the reverse: improve the quality of your rendering, often at the cost of increased rendering time. It is sometimes important to be able to render an image at the highest possible quality and accuracy, for example, when you want to discern very fine details in a data set, like a small artery in an MRI scan of a human heart. A volume visualization application can render a data set at a lower quality and higher speed at first, while the user selects the transfer functions and viewing angle for example. Once the user is satisfied with the settings, the application can go into high-quality mode and rerender the last view to give the user the highest-fidelity image.

Higher Order Interpolation

Typically the volume rendering pipeline uses trilinear interpolation to interpolate voxels. However, from the signal processing literature you might know that linear interpolation is not the best method available. This was discussed in detail in Chapter 5. Linear interpolation introduces smoothing and aliasing. A good higher-order interpolation function to use is the cubic convolution, as we talked about in Chapter 5. The cubic convolution interpolation function operates on 64 voxels in three dimensions, instead of the trilinear interpolation function which operates on 8 voxels. This means that 64 voxels need to be fetched from memory, multiplied with a weighting factor, and added. This will take a lot more computation. However, the cubic convolution interpolation filter is a far better filter than linear interpolation.

Improved Gradient Estimation

Basically the same reasoning as above for interpolation holds for gradient estimation. The central difference gradient operator is certainly not the best operator around. Its biggest drawback is that it sometimes wrongly predicts the direction of a gradient. This has a big impact on the quality of the rendering, since the shading stage in the pipeline depends heavily on the direction of the gradient. We showed an example in Chapter 3. Also, the central difference gradient operator smooths—it misses small and fine details. Often smoothing is aesthetically pleasing to the human eye, but it doesn't necessarily mean that it is correct, in the sense that it truly shows what the data set contains.

You will get a bigger improvement in image quality using a better gradient operator than a higher-order interpolation function. The effects of a better gradient operator are far more noticeable. Thus, if you are considering doing one or the other, first use a better gradient estimator and then use a better interpolation filter.

Oversampling

Oversampling is the term we use to denote taking more sample points on one ray or to cast more rays through a data set. You can also think of this as oversampling in the z-direction, on the ray, and oversampling in the x- and y-direction, on the image plane. Figure 8.9(a) shows oversampling on a ray and Figure 8.9(b) shows oversampling on the image plane. When we oversample on a ray the sampling rate in each major axis should be at least a factor of two to meet the Nyquist criteria. You can prove that using signal processing theory and Fourier analysis. This assumes that you are doing a perfect job of interpolation and gradient estimation, which we never do. Therefore taking even more within a voxel cube is useful.

Since we are working in three dimensions, it also makes sense to oversample in the two other dimensions, not only on the ray. That means casting more rays from the image plane through the data set. We can accomplish this in two ways. First, we can cast rays from points between the pixels on the image plane. However, since a pixel is the smallest dot on the screen, we need to figure out how to deal with the resulting points in between the pixels. Figure 8.10 shows this situation. The dots are the pixels on the screen. We cast a ray from each pixel. The crosses are the points in between the pixels we also cast rays from. This specific example casts four rays per pixel, as shown with the dotted box around the four points. We need to decide how to combine the values we get after compositing for these four rays into one pixel color. One commonly used method is to calculate the average of the four values and assign that value to the pixel. In our example in Figure 8.10 that is the upper-left pixel. Another possibility is to apply a median filter to the four points and use that result. The average filter seems to generate good results.

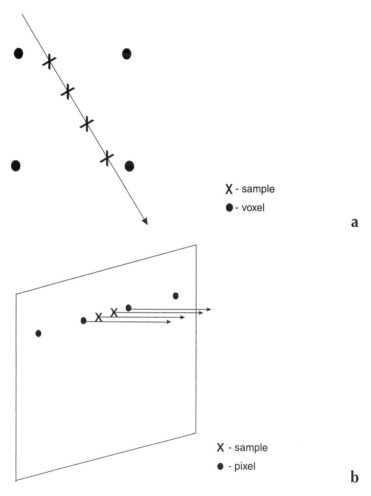

FIGURE 8.9 (a) Oversampling on one ray using four sample points; (b) oversampling on the image plane with two extra rays between the voxels.

Instead of casting rays in between pixels, we can use the transformation matrix, as we described in Chapter 2, to scale the data set up into the x-, y- and z-direction and then start casting rays for each pixel (see Figure 8.11). In Figure 8.11(a) we show the original situation, without oversampling. In Figure 8.11(b) we show the oversampling. The data set is larger and therefore the projection on the

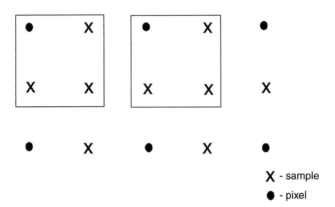

X - sample

● - pixel

FIGURE 8.10 Oversampling by casting more rays between pixels. The four results can be averaged and that result assigned to the upper-left pixel.

image plane is also. We will thus cast more rays through the data set than in Figure 8.11(a). Of course the final image on the image plane will also be bigger, and that can be an undesirable effect. However, you do not have to apply an averaging filter, or any other filter, anymore. Note that both methods will cast the same amount of rays through the data set, if the scaling is the same for each method. The first method needs an additional step and is therefore slightly more compute intensive.

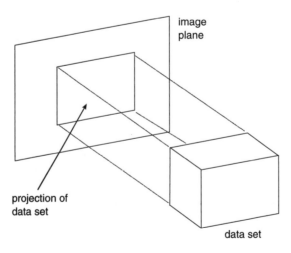

image plane

projection of
data set

data set

FIGURE 8.11(a) Original situation.

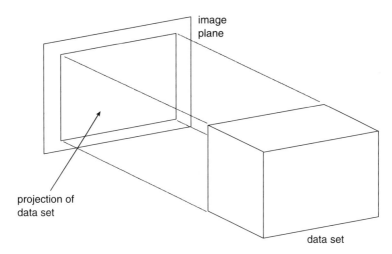

FIGURE 8.11(b) Oversampling by scaling the data set. The projection on the image plane also scales by the same amount.

Interpolation and Classification Order

Earlier we talked of the operation order in our volume rendering pipeline. When computing shaded samples, there are two options. The first is to interpolate or resample first and then classify and assign a color. The second option is to color and classify first and then resample. The color and classify first option has the advantage of being able to precompute the classification and shading if the light sources are fixed and the classification function does not change. Resampling first has the advantage that it tends to convey more information about the three-dimensional structure. Resampling first has the disadvantage that the rendered image may change appearance as the viewing angle changes, because the location of sample points on a ray is viewpoint dependent, and therefore the shading and classification are viewpoint dependent.

SPEEDUP TECHNIQUES

Since volume rendering in software can take a long time, many tricks have been presented in the literature to get away with doing the minimum amount of work possible. We divide the trade-offs that are made to speed up the rendering into two groups. One class of algorithms will trade-off image quality for rendering speed. The other class will preserve the image quality while trying to improve the rendering speed. Of course the latter is preferable, if it achieves the speedups you want. Note that in either case you are almost always making another trade-off: memory for speed. That means that the memory requirements of the algorithm go up, sometimes considerably. This section will briefly discuss some of the more popular speedy algorithms.

Space Leaping by Blocking

By quantifying volume data into a block, statistics of the block may be kept. It is a simple matter and fairly small overhead to keep a running sum of the opacity resulting from classification of voxels within a block. When the sum of opacity values of all voxels within a block falls below a predetermined threshold, it is needless to process that block any further in the volume rendering pipeline since the whole block is transparent. Volume data sets used in a variety of fields are comprised mostly of *empty* space. For example, a medical data set can be far more than 50 percent empty. This practice can provide a tremendous performance boost in rendering these sparse volumes.

On top of blocking often some kind of hierarchical data structure is used. A common data organization is the octree. At each node of the octree you can store some summary information about the data at that node, like an ignore flag. The lowest node will have one block in it, the next higher node will have eight blocks in it, and so on. This allows for skipping bigger regions at a time.

Note that some data sets have hardly any uninteresting data in them at all. This can be the case for a geological data set, as we showed in Chapter 3.

Early Ray Termination

When casting a ray and compositing resultant values along the ray from front to back, another performance benefit can be realized. For a ray, the accumulated opacity value has to be maintained during traversal. When the accumulated opacity value exceeds a predetermined threshold, saturating opacity sufficiently close to 1.0, traversal along the ray can be discontinued. This technique is known as early ray termination. Further sample points along the ray will not contribute anymore since the maximum opacity value is already reached.

Smart Clipping

You obtain the best rendering performance when you actually render the least amount of your volume as possible. A volume can be clipped by either the viewport window (in image space) or by the introduction of additional clipping planes (in model space). Performance benefits are realized if the nonviewable portions of the volume can be identified and eliminated from the rendering process. Identification of clipped blocks can completely eliminate them from further rendering. Nonvisible regions within a block can be eliminated by prescribing the correct beginning and ending points along the cast ray and eliminating the unused portions.

Distance Transform

The distance transform is a preprocessing step before the actual rendering. For each voxel in the data set you compute the distance to the next nearest interesting voxel. This distance is then stored with the voxel. When we render the data set, we use this distance information to skip over data. Once we cast a ray and have processed one voxel on that ray, we know that there are no interesting sample points within a sphere with a radius of that distance. We can start sampling on the ray outside that sphere and start processing again. We show this situation in Figure 8.12. The voxel nearest to the first processed sample point has a distance value of two stored with it. That means that we can advance a length of two over the ray and start sampling again. This is the sample point outside the big circle in Figure 8.12. The voxel nearest to this sample point has a value of one associated with it. This time we advance a length of one over the ray and start processing again. The processed and skipped sample points are marked in the figure.

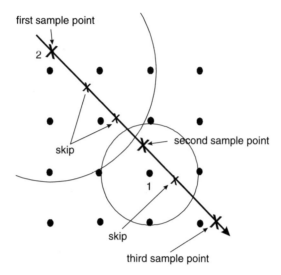

FIGURE 8.12   The distance number at each voxel denotes the distance we can skip on a ray.

Progressive Refinement

One way to speed up the volume rendering is to use progressive refinement. The idea is to trade off image quality for speed as the user is adjusting parameters such as scale or rotation. While the user fine-tunes these parameters, the screen is updated with lower-quality images. These lower-quality images are obtained by rendering a subsampled data set, casting fewer rays through the data set, sampling the rays at a lower frequency, or using a lower quality interpolation method such as nearest neighbor. Implementing one or several of these speedups will show dramatic improvements in rendering speed. When the adjustable parameters are finalized, the image can be rendered in the normal high-image quality manner. Sometimes the two different rendering modes can be determined quite easily. It may be a matter of sensing when a mouse button is depressed as the user drags a slider bar across the screen adjusting the scale factor.

Precalculation of Data

Another technique used to improve rendering speed is precalculation of intermediate data. Depending on which parameters get altered during image viewing, you can preassign the segmentation and classification values as well as precompute the gradient values. The advantage is the speed gained by avoiding duplicate operations. The disadvantage is the memory required to store these intermediate values. You must also monitor the user's input to determine if and when new intermediate values need to be regenerated.

FOR FURTHER STUDY

Hierarchical data structures and progressive refinement are discussed in [133], [135], [112], [261], and [262]. The distance transformation and the related ray acceleration by distance coding technique are explained in detail in [272] and [271].

The For Further Study section in Chapter 3 mentions several gradient and interpolation papers. In [156] you'll find a good discussion on the merits of improving the gradient computation versus the interpolation filter.

In [139] design issues around a complete volume rendering system are discussed, including blocking, bus bandwidth, and software API issues.

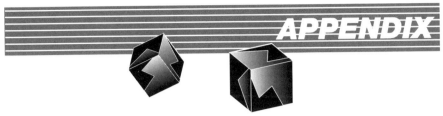

VOLUME RENDERING RESOURCES

This section is by no means exhaustive. Hopefully, it will provide enough information to get you started.

PERIODICALS

Academic Press, Inc.
Journal Division
525 B Street, Suite 1900
San Diego, CA 92101-4495
Tel: (619) 230-1840
Fax: (619) 699-6800

Computer Vision, Graphics and Image Processing: Graphical Models and Image Processing
Computer Vision, Graphics and Image Processing: Image Understanding
Journal of Visual Communication and Image Representation

Advanced Imaging Circulation
445 Broad Hollow Road
Melville, NY 11747-4722

Advanced Imaging

IEEE Services Center
445 Hoes Lane
P.O. Box 1331
Piscataway, NJ 08855-1331
Tel: (212) 705-7900

IEEE Transactions on Image Processing
IEEE Transactions on Medical Imaging
IEEE Transactions on Signal Processing

IEEE Computer Society
10662 Los Vaqueros Circle
P.O. Box 3014
Los Alamitos, CA 90720-1264
Tel: (714) 821-8380

IEEE Transactions on Computer Graphics and Applications

Association for Computing Machinery Special Interest Group for
     Graphics
P.O. Box 12114
Church Street Station
New York, NY 10257
Tel: (212) 626-0500
Fax: (212) 944-1318

SIGGRAPH Conference Proceedings

EUROGRAPHICS Association
P.O. Box 16
CH-1288 Aire-la-Ville
Switzerland
Fax: +41-22-757.0318

Computer Graphics Forum

ORGANIZATIONS AND CONFERENCES

DSP Associates
49 River Street
Waltham, MA 02154
Tel: (617) 891-6000
Fax: (617) 899-4449
E-mail: icspat@dspnet.com

International Conference on Signal Processing Applications & Technology

The International Society for Optical Engineering
P.O. Box 10
Bellingham, WA 98227-0010
Tel: (360) 676-3290
Fax: (360) 647-1445
email: spie@spie.org

SPIE's International Symposium Medical Imaging
IS&T/SPIE's Symposium on Electronic Imaging: Science & Technology

The Society for Imaging Science and Technology
7003 Kilworth Lane
Springfield, VA 22151
Tel: (703) 642-9090
Fax: (703) 642-9094

IS&T/SPIE's Symposium on Electronic Imaging: Science & Technology

International Association of Science and Technology Development
P.O. Box 25, Station G
Calgary, AB, Canada T3A 2G1
Tel: (403) 270-3616

IASTED International Conference Signal and Image Processing

Institute of Electrical and Electronics Engineers
345 East 47th Street
New York, NY 10017-2394
Tel: (212) 705-7900

IEEE International Conference on Image Processing
IEEE Visualization Conference
Image & Multidimensional Signal Processing Workshop

IEEE Computer Society
10662 Los Vaqueros Circle
P.O. Box 3014
Los Alamitos, CA 90720-1264
Tel: (714) 821-8380

International Conference on Computer Vision
IEEE Computer Society Conference on Computer Vision and Pattern
    Recognition

Association for Computing Machinery Special Interest Group for
    Graphics
P.O. Box 12114
Church Street Station
New York, NY 10257
Tel: (212) 626-0500
Fax: (212) 944-1318

ACM SIGGRAPH Conference

National Computer Graphics Association
2722 Merrilee Drive, Suite 200
Fairfax, Va 22031-4499
Tel: (703) 698-9600
Fax: (703) 560-2752

NCGA Conference and Exposition

EUROGRAPHICS Association
P.O. Box 16
CH-1288 Aire-la-Ville
Switzerland
Fax: +41-22-757.0318

Eurographics Conference

INTERNET RESOURCES

The Internet provides an unlimited source of data sets, programs, and information about volume rendering.

When we compiled this resource section, we debated whether to include Internet resources. Internet servers and addresses appear and disappear overnight. If we did include this information, some of it would be outdated by the time the book was printed. We still felt that the benefits of including this information far outweighed the drawbacks.

Usenet Newsgroups

Newsgroups are forums for discussions on specific topics. There are thousands of these groups available on the internet. We've listed the ones that are the most appropriate for someone interested in volume rendering.

alt.image.medical	Imaging in the medical community
comp.dsp	Digital signal processing
comp.graphics.algorithms	Raster and vector graphics algorithms
comp.graphics.research	Latest graphics research
comp.graphics.visualization	Scientific visualization
comp.sys.mac.scitech	Macintosh scientific applications
sci.image.processing	Image processing and image analysis

World Wide Web Sites

On the CD-Rom is a collection of our favorite volume rendering URLs. They are all in the file VR.html. These Web sites are included because they show what different organizations and companies are doing with volume rendering. Some sites show research efforts; others have downloadable data sets that you can render; still others show some of their commercial products.

Data Sets

Besides the data sets available on the CD-ROM, you may want to look at the following.

UMDS IPG Medical Image Archive. —You can download multiple modality data sets: CT, MR, and PET. Find them at http://www-ipg.umds.ac.uk/archive.html (This URL is included in the bookmarks file on the CD.)

MRI Monkey Head Data Set. —Dr. Masato Taira at Nihon University created this data set via MRI. Anonymous ftp it from ftp.nc.nihon-u.ac.jp in /pub/data/MRIMonkeyHead/.

Chapel Hill Volume Data Set. —MRI and CT scans of brains, heads, and knees are available via ftp. Go to omicron.cs.unc.edu in directory pub/projects/softlab.v/CHVRTD. The actual directory has moved around over the years. If you don't find it immediately, look in the index file. They are probably still there. Each data set comes with its own .info file detailing the dimensions of the data set.

SEARCHABLE DATABASES

SIGGRAPH On-line Bibliography Project

This database contains thousands of references to computer graphics and image processing books and articles. Though information can be obtained via FTP or by logging on, the best method is to log on to siggraph.org with a login of biblio. You may then search the database for keywords or authors. For information on how to conduct a search, type ? or h for help. A typical search consists of a **find** command followed by the **display** command.

sci.image.processing Archive

This database stores all articles posted to sci.image.processing. Access to these articles is by way of an almanac mail server. Send a mail message to almanac@ruby.oce.orst.edu. In the message body include the line

search sci.image.processing keyword

where keyword is the search keyword or set of keywords. You will receive the results of the search by E-mail as a list of article numbers and subjects. Select the subjects of interest and retrieve those articles. Articles are retrieved by sending a retrieve request to the almanac mail server. The format is

retrieve sci.image.processing article_number

Your retrieve request may request numerous articles and may also be mixed with search commands. You may also retrieve the articles via FTP to ruby.oce.orst.edu from the directory /pub/sci.image.processing. This method requires that you already know the number of the article you wish to retrieve.

PUBLIC DOMAIN SOFTWARE

These programs are free or close to it. Some require the cost of the media they are shipped on.

Vis5D

Vis5D is an interactive visualization program that runs on HP, Sun, IBM, DEC, and SGI workstations. It will also run on PC compatibles running Linux version 1.2 or later. You can get it via anonymous ftp from iris.ssec.wisc.edu in pub/vis5d. The distribution consists of two files. The file vis5d-4.2.tar.Z contains the source code and documentation. The second file, vis5d-data.tar.Z, contains data sets. You can also get precompiled Vis5D executables. For more information, visit http://www.ssec.wisc.edu/~billh/vis5d.html.

VolVis

VolVis is a volume rendering package that runs on HP, Sun, and SGI workstations. To find out how to get VolVis, go to http://www.cs.sunyb.edu/~volvis.

VolPack

VolPack is a software library of volume rendering components. It is available by anonymous ftp from graphics.stanford.edu in the pub/volpack directory.

BOB(GVLware)

BOB is an interactive volume renderer available via anonymous ftp from ftp.arc.umn.edu in /pub/GVL/gvl.tar.Z. Source and precompiled binaries are available.

ROSS

ROSS stands for Reconstruction of Serial Sections. This software works with 3D serial section reconstruction (confocal microscopy, CT, and MR imaging). To find out how to get it, visit http://biocomp.arc.nasa.gov.ross.

Dr. Razz

Dr. Razz is a program for the Macintosh. It is optimized for display of CT and MR images. It is available via ftp from fttp.u.washington.edu/pub/user-supported/razz/.

KHOROS

Khoros is a data processing and analysis tool. It is very powerful and also very large (100 megabytes). It has a graphical interface and an extensive library of image and signal processing routines. It is written for Unix systems running X11 windows. You may ftp it from *ftp.khoral.com* in /pub/khoros.

NIH Image

This is an image and volume processing for the Macintosh. It can acquire, display, process, and print images. Image processing abilities include contrast enhancement, edge detection, filtering, and convolutions (kernel sizes up to 63x63). NIH has a macro programming language that allows automating complex and repetitive tasks. It also supports Adobe Photoshop compatible plug-ins. NIH can be obtained via ftp from *zippy.nimh.nih.gov* in the pub/nih-image directory. For more information, visit http://rsb.info.nih.gov/nih-image/.

OSIRIS

OSIRIS is a general medical imaging package that runs on most workstations as well as PCs running Windows 3.1 or NT. It can be obtained free of charge from

Digital Imaging Unit
University Hospital of Geneva
24 Micheli du Crest
1211 Geneva 14 - Switzerland
Fax (+41 22) 327 61 98
E-mail:osiris@dim.hcuge.ch

For more information on OSIRIS, see http://expasy.hcuge.ch/www/UIN/html/projects/osiris/osiris.html.

3DVIEWNIX

3DVIEWNIX is transportable software developed by the Medical Image Processing Group at the University of Pennsylvania. It was designed to analyze, manipulate, and visualize multidimensional multimodality image information. It runs under X-windows on HP, Sun, SGI, and IBM workstations. For more information contact

Prof. J.K. Udupa
Medical Image Processing Group
Department of Radiology
University of Pennsylvania
418 Service Drive - 4th floor Blockley Hall
Philadelphia, PA 19104-6021
Phone: (215) 662-6780
FAX: (215) 898-9145
E-mail: Vhelp@mipg.upenn.edu
www: http://www.mipg.upenn.edu

VFLEET

VFleet is a color volume renderer. It can handle very large data sets and runs on UNIX platforms. VFleet was developed at the Pittsburgh Supercomputing center. You can find more information at http://www.pscinfo.psc.edu/software/packages/vfleet/vfleet.html.

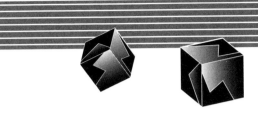

VOLUME RENDERING EXTENSIONS FOR OPENGL®

TABLE OF CONTENTS

INTRODUCTION

This document describes a set of API entry points that extend OpenGL to perform high-quality volume rendering. All comments on this specification should be directed via E-mail to either *voxelator@fc.hp.com* (comments are received only by HP) or to *voxelator-public@fc.hp.com* (comments are received by everyone on the Voxelator public discussion list).

Version 4.00—August 1, 1997. Copyright © 1996, 1997 Hewlett-Packard Company.

There are several significant reasons for proposing this API and soliciting feedback from leaders in volume rendering. We believe OpenGL will become the visualization API of choice for the majority of application developers. Our discussions with potential customers have led us to believe that OpenGL does not currently contain the capabilities necessary to perform high-quality volume rendering. This specification is our attempt to define those capabilities within OpenGL in a way that supports applications development and allows a wide variety of hardware acceleration schemes.

Figure 1 is a simplified diagram of the current OpenGL state machine that shows the two rendering pipelines that exist today. The one most familiar to people is the geometry pipeline. The geometry pipeline accepts vertex commands that define geometric primitives and then performs transformation, lighting, shading, clipping, and rasterization of these primitives. The geometry pipeline

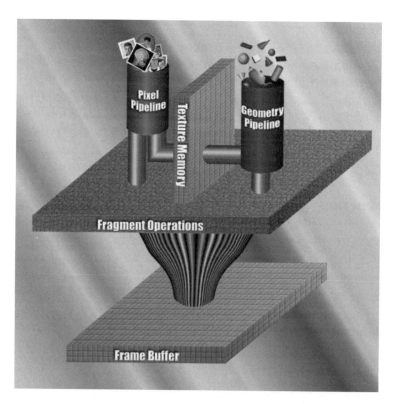

FIGURE 1 Simplified diagram of the OpenGL rendering environment.

produces fragments (data structures that define the values necessary to update a pixel location in the frame buffer). Fragments are subjected to a variety of tests known as fragment operations. The fragment operations produce a sequence of frame buffer updates.

A somewhat overlooked feature of the OpenGL rendering environment is the pixel pipeline. The pixel pipeline has been significantly enhanced with extensions that are supported by SGI and HP, including scale and bias operations, look-up table operations, and convolution. One of the two paths through the pixel pipeline allows images to be processed by the pipeline, rasterized, subjected to the fragment operations, and sent to the frame buffer immediately. The other path through the pixel pipeline allows images to be processed by the pixel processing stages of the pipeline and stored in texture memory for later use by the geometry pipeline. Notice that once

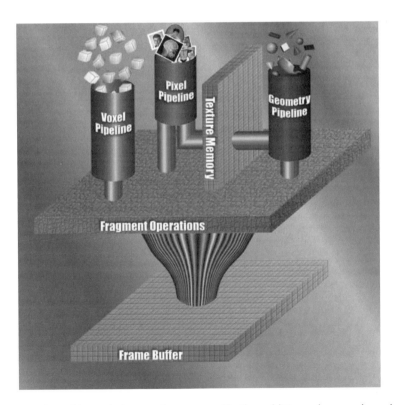

FIGURE 2 OpenGL rendering environment with the addition of a voxel rendering pipeline.

fragments are generated by either the geometry or the pixel pipeline, all further processing is identical.

Figure 2 shows a new pipeline for OpenGL that supports volume rendering—a voxel pipeline. This pipeline has its own set of pipeline stages that are shown pictorially in Figure 3 and are defined in the remainder of this document. This third pipeline is affected by some of the state that affects the geometry pipeline (for instance, transformation, lighting, and model clipping attributes), but several new state values are also defined. This pipeline produces fragments that are exactly the same as those produced by the other two pipelines, and the generated fragments are processed by the fragment operations in an identical manner.

In the text that follows, the stages of the voxel pipeline will be presented in the order they occur. Entry points that are defined by this specification contain the suffix "HP" to differentiate them from core OpenGL routines and a "glVR" prefix to clearly indicate that they apply to the volume rendering pipeline.

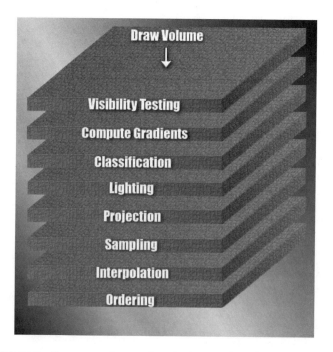

FIGURE 3   Sequence of operations in the voxel rendering pipeline.

TERMINOLOGY

A *volume data set* is a three-dimensional array of voxels. A volume data set usually contains values that have been obtained by some type of 3D scanning or sampling device. After acquisition, these values may be further modified either by an automatic process (such as performing a filtering operation to remove noise) or by a manual process (such as determining which voxels represent similar materials and labeling them accordingly). *Volume rendering* is the process of turning this data into an image, and the *voxel pipeline* is the sequence of operations that occur during the volume rendering process.

The word "voxel" comes from combining the words "volume element" in the same way that the words "picture element" are combined to form the word "pixel." Each voxel consists of a position and a value. The *voxel position* is a three-tuple that specifies a position within the three-dimensional voxel array. The *origin* of the volume data set is considered to be the center of the very first voxel [i.e., the voxel with coordinates (0,0,0)]. The first coordinate of the voxel position represents the column, the second coordinate represents the row, and the third coordinate represents the image (or *slice*). Columns, rows, and images are numbered starting from 0. The voxel in the 23rd column, 45th row, and 15th image would have a position of (22, 44, 14). In order to allow more efficient processing, volume data sets are organized into chunks called *blocks.*

The *voxel value* may consist of one or more elements, depending on the *voxel format.* Voxel values may have an *intensity* element, which is simply a scalar value that has been measured or assigned to that voxel location. They may also have an *index* element. If present, the index portion of the voxel value can be used to "label" voxel locations as containing material of a certain type. The intensity and index components are treated separately during the volume rendering process in order to achieve useful visualization effects. In cases where a preprocessing step has already assigned color values to voxel locations, each voxel value may contain a color element consisting of red, green, blue, and possibly alpha components. Finally, if gradients have been computed by a preprocessing step, each voxel value may also contain a gradient consisting of *x*, *y*, and *z* components.

CAPABILITY QUERIES

This section describes the implementation-dependent constants that affect the voxel pipeline. These values may be queried with the standard OpenGL *glGet* function.

The *volume data definition section* (below) describes how blocks are defined and used in this API. The following values should be queried by an application prior to organizing a volume data set into blocks:

- GL_VR_OPTIMAL_BLOCK_WIDTH_EXT
- GL_VR_OPTIMAL_BLOCK_HEIGHT_EXT
- GL_VR_OPTIMAL_BLOCK_DEPTH_EXT

The values returned for these tokens specify the dimensions of the optimal block for the underlying implementation. Volume data sets that are formatted using the optimal block width, height, and depth have the best chance of taking full advantage of hardware acceleration.

Block dimensions are not restricted to powers of two, but it might be common to find that the dimensions of the optimal block size are powers of two.

The *lighting section* describes how lights are used in the voxel pipeline. In order to determine the capabilities of the lighting stage of the voxel pipeline, applications should query the value of the constant:

- GL_VR_MAX_LIGHTS_EXT

The lighting stage of the volume rendering pipeline uses the current OpenGL lighting state. However, the implementation may not support as many light sources for volume rendering as are defined for geometry. This token allows you to query the maximum number of light sources that may be used when rendering volumes.

The *classification section* describes how intensity and gradient values are used to assign red, green, blue, and alpha values. The classification stage of the pipeline allows the magnitude of the gradient to be used as part of the look-up table index. In order to determine the number of bits in the gradient magnitude, applications should query the value of the constant:

- GL_VR_GRADIENT_MAGNITUDE_BITS_EXT

VOLUME DATA DEFINITION

In order to allow more efficient processing, volume data sets must be passed as a collection of blocks. Before passing any volume data, applications must use the following procedure to specify the size of the blocks that will be used:

```
GLvoid glVRBlockSizeEXT
        (GLsizei          blockwidth,
         GLsizei          blockheight,
         GLsizei          blockdepth)
```

blockwidth	width of a block (in voxels)
blockheight	height of a block (in voxels)
blockdepth	depth of a block (in voxels)

Each block will contain the voxel values that make up a sub-volume of the overall volume. The voxel values in a block are organized linearly in memory. A block does *not* include any overlap with adjacent blocks. *glVRBlockSizeEXT* is used to specify the block size that will be used to supply volume data for rendering. The width, height, and depth of the optimal block should be determined by making queries with *glGet* and these values should be used if at all possible. The default value for each of these attributes is 16. If the desired block size differs from the defaults, the block size must be set prior to calling either *glVRVolumeDataEXT* or *glVRVoxel-MaskEXT*.

A volume data set is defined with the following command:

```
GLvoid glVRVolumeDataEXT
          (GLsizei         width,
          GLsizei          height,
          GLsizei          depth,
          GLenum           format,
          const GLvoid*    *blockptrs)
```

width	width of the volume data set (in voxels)
height	height of the volume data set (in voxels)
depth	depth of the volume data set (in voxels)
format	format of voxels in the volume data set
blockptrs	array containing pointers to blocks in the volume data set

This call is used to define a volume data set. Applications are required to arrange the volume data set in memory as a series of blocks, define a list of pointers to these blocks by calling *glVRVolumeDataEXT*, and then call *glVRDrawVolumeEXT* to provide the data to OpenGL. Data sets must be padded so that their dimensions are an even multiple of the block dimensions. The size of the data set (in voxels) is specified by *width, height,* and *depth*. The *blockptrs* argument specifies an array of pointers to the blocks that comprise the data set. The number of pointers in the array is the number of blocks in the data set. Since *width, height,* and *depth* must be multiples of *blockwidth, blockheight,* and *blockdepth,* respectively, this can be computed by taking (*width/blockwidth*) * (*height/blockheight*) * (*depth/blockheight*). The pointer array is not accessed until *glVRDrawVolumeEXT* is called. A pointer value of NULL indicates an empty block (i.e., a block that contains no data). The format of the data is specified by *format,* which may be one of

- GL_INTENSITY8_EXT
- GL_INTENSITY16_EXT
- GL_INDEX4_INTENSITY12_EXT
- GL_INDEX8_INTENSITY8_EXT

- GL_INDEX16_INTENSITY16_EXT
- GL_RGBA8888_EXT
- GL_INTENSITY8_XYZ888_EXT
- GL_INTENSITY8_RGB888_EXT

The number of bits for each component is encoded in the format name. Gradient components (XYZ) are signed; all other components are unsigned.

The voxel values that are provided are organized in such a way that each voxel's position can be determined implicitly. The very first voxel in the data set is assumed to be at voxel position (0,0,0). This voxel position is also assumed to be the origin of the volume data set. The second voxel in the data set is assumed to be at voxel position (1,0,0), the third at (2,0,0), and so on. Figure 4 shows some of the voxels in a volume data set that contains *width x height x depth* voxels. The voxel centered at the origin has a voxel location

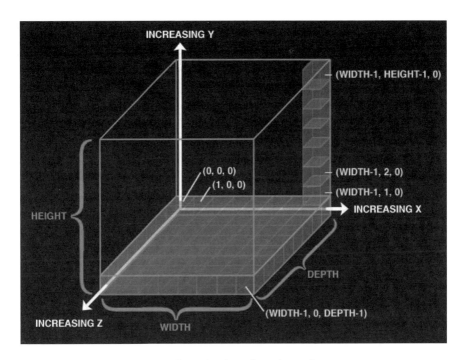

FIGURE 4   Organization of a volume data set.

of (0,0,0). The next voxel has a location of (1,0,0). The X coordinate continues to increase to the right in the diagram, until the end of the first row is reached. This voxel has a voxel location of (width-1, 0, 0). The voxel directly above this one is at the end of the second row, and its location is (width-1, 1, 0). Above this one is the voxel with location (width-1, 2, 0). The last voxel of the first slice has a voxel location of (width-1, height-1, 0). This sequence continues with each successive slice of the volume data set.

The number of pointers in the array is passed in the numptrs parameter and the pointers themselves are passed in *blockptrs*. Several utilities are provided to construct these voxel blocks. For best results, applications should query the optimal block width, height, and depth as described above and then organize their data set according to the values that are returned.

Figure 5 shows the location of six of the blocks in a volume data set that happens to be four blocks wide. The first pointer in the

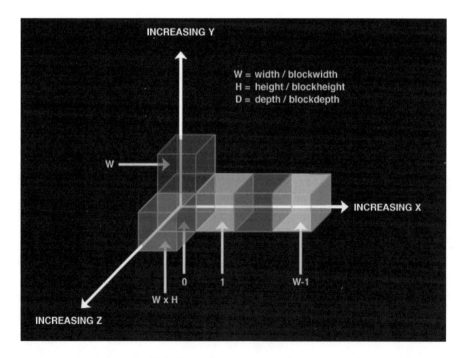

FIGURE 5 Organization of blocks within a volume data set (an example where the data set happens to be four blocks wide).

blockptrs array points to the block that contains the origin of the volume data set [i.e., the voxel with coordinates (0,0,0)]. In the diagram, this block is mostly obscured by blocks on either side and on top. This first block (block number 0) will contain the voxels whose positions range from [0,*blockwidth*-1] in X, [0,*blockheight*-1] in Y, and [0,*blockdepth*-1] in Z. The second block (block number 1) is the yellow one in the diagram, and it will contain the voxels whose positions range from [*blockwidth*,2*blockwidth-1] in X, [0,*block-height*-1] in Y, and [0,*blockdepth*-1] in Z. This sequence continues through block number W-1, where W=*width/blockwidth*, shown as a gray block in the diagram. The next block in the sequence is block number W (the red block), and the sequence continues until block W × H − 1 is reached. A new sequence of blocks is started with block W × H (shown as the green block in the diagram), and the pattern is followed for the remaining blocks in the volume data set.

Voxel values in each block are stored as a one-dimensional array. The first voxel value in each block is the voxel whose position is closest to the origin of the volume data set. Voxel positions are used to determine the order of the remainder of the voxels within the block. Once again, the first coordinate varies fastest, then the second coordinate, and then the third.

An INVALID_VALUE error will be generated if *width* is not an even multiple of *blockwidth*, or if *height* is not an even multiple of *blockheight*, or if *depth* is not an even multiple of *blockdepth*. If the contribution of a particular voxel depends on the computation of gradients and voxel values at neighboring voxels and those neighboring voxels do not exist (e.g., voxels at an edge of the volume or adjacent to a block that is skipped), then the voxel in question is not rendered. If it is necessary to consider the contribution of voxels along the edges of the volume data set, it is up to the application to add additional voxels to the edges in order to achieve the desired rendering effect.

Each block has a particular action attribute that can be set with the following routine:

```
GLvoid glVRBlockActionsEXT
        (const GLenum    *actions)
```

actions   array containing an action token for each block

The *actions* array contains one entry for each block in the volume data set that is to be rendered. Values in the array are not accessed until *glVRDrawVolumeEXT* is called. The number of entries in the arrays is determined at the time *glVRDrawVolumeEXT* is called by computing (*width/blockwidth*) * (*height/blockheight*) * (*depth/blockheight*). Each value in the *actions* array may be one of

```
GL_VR_RENDER_UNCOMPRESSED_EXT
GL_VR_RENDER_RLE_COMPRESSED_EXT
GL_VR_SKIP_EXT
```

Blocks with an action of GL_VR_RENDER_UNCOMPRESSED_EXT are assumed to contain uncompressed volume data and will be rendered normally. Blocks with an action of GL_VR_RENDER_RLE_COMPRESSED_EXT are assumed to contain RLE compressed volume data and will be decompressed and then rendered normally. Blocks with an action of GL_VR_SKIP_EXT will not be rendered or processed in any way.

If the block attributes are not specified, each block is treated as though it has a defined action of GL_VR_RENDER_UNCOMPRESSED_EXT. The format of RLE compressed blocks is TBD.

DRAWING A VOLUME

A volume data set is sent to the voxel pipeline for processing with the command

```
GLvoid glVRDrawVolumeEXT
     (GLboolean  cachedData)
```

cachedData   Boolean that indicates whether cached data is to be generated/used

Once a volume data set has been defined by *glVRVolumeDataEXT*, it may be rendered by calling *glVRDrawVolumeEXT*. This causes the currently defined volume data set to be traversed and rendered with the current set of rendering attributes, including the block attributes specified by *glVRBlockActionsEXT*. If *cached-*

Data is TRUE, the implementation is permitted to use intermediate results from the previous call to *glVRDrawVolumeEXT,* as long as there have been no intervening calls to *glVRDrawSlice, glVRVolumeDataEXT,* or *glVRBlockSizeEXT.* In addition, the implementation is instructed to generate whatever intermediate results might improve the performance of subsequent renderings. If c*achedData* is FALSE, any cached results will be ignored, no intermediate results will be generated, and the volume data set will be rerendered in its entirety.

The *glVRDrawSliceEXT* function can be used to render an arbitrary slice of the volume data set:

```
GLvoid glVRDrawSliceEXT
        (const GLdouble  *equation
        GLboolean        cachedData)
```

equation	pointer to a vector of four values that define a plane equation
cachedData	Boolean that indicates whether cached data is to be generated/used

This function causes the specified plane to be intersected with the current volume data set, and only the voxels that contribute to the rendering of this plane will be rendered. The *equation* argument is a pointer to four values that are interpreted as the four components of a plane equation. The components of the plane equation are transformed by the inverse of the modelview matrix into eye coordinates. If c*achedData* is TRUE, the implementation is permitted to use intermediate results from the previous call to *glVRDrawVolumeEXT* or *glVRDrawSlice,* as long as there have been no intervening calls to *glVRVolumeDataEXT* or *glVRBlockSizeEXT.* In addition, the implementation is instructed to generate whatever intermediate results might improve the performance of subsequent renderings. If c*achedData* is FALSE, any cached results will be ignored, no intermediate results will be generated, and the volume data set will be rerendered in its entirety.

VISIBILITY TESTING

Two methods are provided for rapidly defining parts of the volume to be invisible (i.e., the final alpha value is forced to zero). It should be noted that the boundary between visible/invisible volume data is handled differently than the boundary between regions where data is present and those where no data is present. Boundaries between regions of data/no data occur (a) at the boundaries of the volume data set and (b) at the boundaries between blocks that are rendered and those that are skipped. In the case of the visible/invisible boundary, interpolation is performed normally between the visible data and the adjoining data (whose final alpha value is forced to zero). In the case of the data/no data boundary, voxels are not rendered if they require gradients and voxel values at neighboring voxels and those neighboring voxels do not exist.

The first method of defining a region to be invisible is with the OpenGL model clip planes. Each voxel location is tested against each enabled model clip plane. If the dot product of the eye coordinates of a voxel location and an enabled model clip plane equation is positive or zero, the voxel location is "in" with respect to that clipping plane; otherwise it is "out." If a voxel location is "out" with respect to any clipping plane, its alpha value is forced to zero and the classification step defined below is not applied. Since the data is not discarded (as it is in the geometry pipeline) we are careful not to refer to this as a clipping operation. The model clipping planes are simply used to define the regions that are visible and those that are invisible. Model clipping planes are enabled/disabled by calling *glEnable/glDisable* with the constant GL_CLIP_PLANEi, where *i* is the number of the plane to be enabled/disabled.

The second method, called the voxel mask test, allows voxel-by-voxel determination of visibility. If the voxel mask test is disabled, all voxels are passed on to the next stage of the voxel processing pipeline. If the voxel mask test is enabled, voxels that are extracted from memory are passed on for further processing only if the corresponding bit in the current voxel mask is set to GL_TRUE. The voxel mask test may be enabled/disabled by calling *glEnable/glDisable* with the constant GL_VR_VOXEL_MASK_TEST_EXT. The voxel mask consists of an array of pointers, each of which specifies a three-dimensional bit field. The pointer array is ordered in the same way as the array passed to *glVRVolumeDataEXT*, and each pointer in the array references a bitfield which will be used to perform visibility testing on the voxels specified by the pointer in the corresponding location in the array passed to *glVRVolumeDataEXT*. The current voxel mask is set by calling *glVRVoxelMaskEXT*, which is defined as follows:

```
GLvoid glVRVoxelMaskEXT
        (GLvoid*           *blockptrs)
```

blockptrs   array containing pointers to bitfields

Each entry in the *blockptrs* array contains a pointer to a bitfield that will be used to perform visibility testing on the corresponding block of voxels. The bits in each bitfield are assumed to be organized in groups of 16 (i.e., stored in 16-bit unsigned integers) and are in the same order as the corresponding voxels. A voxel is considered masked if the corresponding bit in the voxel mask is a 0 and will be rendered normally if the corresponding bit in the voxel mask is a 1. The least significant bit of the first group should indicate whether the voxel at location (0,0,0) is to be masked. The next bit should indicate whether the voxel at location (1,0,0) is to be masked, and so on until the bit corresponding to (*blockwidth*-1,0,0) has been specified. If *blockwidth* is greater than 16, multiple bit groups are used. If *blockwidth* is not evenly divisible by 16, the last group will be padded with unspecified bits. Subsequent bit groups are used to define the remaining rows in the first slice (up to *blockheight*-1), and then the remaining slices in the block (up to *blockdepth*-1).

Values in the *blockptrs* array are not accessed until *glVRDrawVolumeEXT* is called. The number of entries in the array is determined at the time *glVRDrawVolumeEXT* is called by computing (*width/blockwidth*) * (*height/blockheight*) * (*depth/blockheight*). A pointer value of NULL indicates that there is no bitfield for the block, and the block should be rendered with all voxels considered visible. If the current voxel mask is smaller than the volume data set that it is being applied to, it is as if the voxel mask were extended in each direction with GL_TRUE bits. The voxel mask test is disabled by default, and the default voxel mask array pointer is NULL.

COMPUTE GRADIENTS

After the visibility test, each voxel that contains an intensity component must have a gradient computed. This stage is skipped when the voxel format contains no intensity component. It is also skipped when the voxel format contains an explicit gradient value.

Not all volume data sets are isotropic. In fact, it is very common for sampling to occur at one resolution in X and Y, and at a different resolution in Z. To allow an implementation to properly compute gradients, applications must supply the scaling factors that are used to convert a nonisotropic volume data set into an isotropic one. To do this, the *glVRScaleFactorsEXT* routine is used:

```
GLvoid glVRScaleFactorsEXT
        (GLfloat        x,
         GLfloat        y,
         GLfloat        z)
```

x scale factor for X axis
y scale factor for Y axis
z scale factor for Z axis

The gradient for each voxel is performed by computing the central difference using the intensity of the current voxel and the intensities of its six nearest neighbors. The equations used to compute a gradient using the central difference method are as follows, where S_x represents the X scaling factor, S_y represents the Y scaling factor, and S_z represents the Z scaling factor:

The default scale factor is 1.0 for each of x, y, and z.

CLASSIFICATION

The process that assigns color (red, green, and blue) and opacity (alpha) values to each voxel location is called classification. Classification is performed by computing an index value that is used to look up red, green, blue, and alpha values in a new color table—

the classification color table. Classification is only performed on voxel values that contain an intensity component.

The values in the classification lookup table are specified by calling *glColorTableEXT* with a target parameter of GL_VR_CLASSI-FICATION_TABLE_EXT. Although other values are permitted, specifying a format of GL_RGBA and an internal_format of GL_RGBA8_EXT or GL_RGBA16_EXT is the most straightforward way to obtain correct results on an implementation that supports a classification table with 2^{16} entries. The classification lookup table can be enabled or disabled by calling *glEnable* or *glDisable* with the value GL_VR_CLASSIFICATION_TABLE_EXT.

By default, the voxel value's intensity component is used as the basis for computing the index into the classification color table. To compute the actual index for the classification table, the voxel value's intensity component is ANDed with the value $2^n - 1$, where 2^n represents the number of entries in the classification lookup table.

A more flexible method for creating the lookup table index is also available. This more flexible method of computing the index can be enabled/disabled by calling *glEnable* or *glDisable* with the value GL_VR_COMPUTE_TABLE_INDEX_EXT. If this mode is enabled, the classification table index value will be computed by combining the voxel value's index component (if present), its intensity value, and the magnitude of the gradient at the voxel location.

When this mode is enabled, the index into the classification lookup table is computed in the following manner. First, the incoming voxel value's intensity component is shifted by GL_VR_INTENSITY_SHIFT_EXT bits to the right. The j bits that remain after this shift are placed in the low-order j bits of the lookup table index. Next, the gradient magnitude that has been computed by the implementation will be shifted GL_VR_GRADIENT_MAGNITUDE _SHIFT_EXT bits to the right. (The number of bits in the gradient magnitude can be queried by calling *glGet* with a *pname* of GL_VR_GRADIENT_MAGNITUDE_BITS_EXT.) The k bits that remain after this shift are placed in the next lowest order k bits of the lookup table index (i.e., bits j to $j+k-1$). Finally, the incoming index value (if there is one) is shifted by GL_VR_INDEX_SHIFT_EXT bits to the right. The m bits that remain after this shift are placed in the next

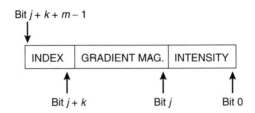

FIGURE 6 Computation of the classification table index.

lowest order m bits of the lookup table index (i.e., bits $j+k$ to $j+k+m-1$). Figure 6 shows the lookup table index as it would appear at this stage.

The final index into the lookup table is computed by ANDing the base index value with the value 2^n-1, where 2^n represents the number of entries in the classification lookup table. Any of the shift values can be set by calling *glVRClassificationParameterEXT*, and the default value for each of them is 0.

```
GLvoid glVRClassificationParameteriEXT
        (GLenum          pname,
         GLint           param)
```

pname   name of parameter to be modified
param   new value for the specified parameter

LIGHTING

Once the base color for the sample point has been determined, the OpenGL RGBA lighting equation is applied, using the gradient as the surface normal and taking the other parameters necessary for the lighting equation from the current material properties and current lighting state. Applying the lighting equation yields final values for R, G, and B. The only difference between the lighting equation for voxels and that used for geometry is that the maximum number of light sources might be different. The maximum number of light sources available for lighting voxels can be determined by calling *glGet* with the constant GL_VR_MAX_LIGHTS_EXT.

PROJECTION

OpenGL's current modelview and projection matrices are used to transform each voxel in the same way that 3D geometry is transformed in OpenGL. The origin of the volume is defined to be the center of the voxel with voxel coordinates (0,0,0) (i.e., the voxel in the lower-left-hand corner of the first image). If the volume to be rendered is w voxels wide, h voxels high, and d voxels deep, it will be transformed as if it were a rectangular solid with modeling coordinates of (0,0,0) at the origin and $(w-1.0, h-1.0, d-1.0)$ at the center of the voxel at the diagonally opposite corner.

Following the application of the modelview and projection matrices, voxel coordinates are transformed into window coordinates by applying the current OpenGL viewport transformation values. These values are specified by calling *glViewport.*

A modeling transformation should be concatenated onto the current modelview matrix in order to properly transform an anisotropic data set. For instance, if a 256×256×128 data set actually represents a real volume with equal dimensions along each side, a modeling matrix that scales the third dimension by a factor of two could be applied in order to display the data set with equal dimensions along each side.

SAMPLING

At this stage of the pipeline, each voxel contains a color (RGBA) value and a location in window coordinates. The RGBA color for each voxel is not rendered directly. Instead, a set of sample points are generated and the RGBA value from the voxel(s) nearest the sample point are used to determine the RGBA value for the sample point. The current sampling frequency value is used to determine the location of the sample points that are computed within the volume. Since interpolation and subsequent rendering computations are performed for each sample point, this attribute has a large impact on rendering performance.

The number of pixels in the projected image of the rendered volume data set determines the number of samples required in the X

and *Y* dimensions. The number of samples to be taken in the *Z* dimension can be specified using the *glVRSamplingFreqEXT* function. The sampling frequency is specified as the number of samples per unit distance in modeling coordinates. The default value for the sampling frequency is 1. There may be either performance or image quality reasons for modifying the current sampling frequency.

```
GLvoid glVRSamplingFreqEXT
    (GLfloat        freq)
```

freq   sampling frequency for the *Z* dimension

Implementations are required to use the sampling frequency as specified for parallel projections. For perspective projections, the sampling frequency must be used where the viewing axis intersects the volume data set, but an approximation of the current sampling frequency may be used for samples that occur off the viewing axis.

INTERPOLATION

Each unclipped sample point requires the computation of a color (RGBA) value. The color values of the nearest voxel(s) are used to estimate the color at the sample point. If the current interpolation method is GL_NEAREST, the color of the voxel nearest the sample point will be used as the color of the sample point. If the current interpolation method is GL_LINEAR, the color values of the eight nearest voxels are used and a trilinear weighting is performed to determine the color of the sample point.

The current interpolation method can be set by calling glVRInterpMethodEXT with one of the values GL_NEAREST or GL_LINEAR. The default value is GL_NEAREST.

```
GLvoid glVRInterpMethodEXT
    (GLenum        method)
```

method   interpolation method to be used

ORDERING

At this point in the rendering pipeline, each sample point has a computed window coordinate and RGBA value. Each sample point generates a fragment. All of the fragments that contribute to a specific pixel location will be rendered according to the current compositing order, which may be one of

- GL_BACK_TO_FRONT_EXT
- GL_FRONT_TO_BACK_EXT

In order to combine all of the sample points that contribute to a particular fragment, some intermediate storage may be required. Allocation and deallocation of this storage is the responsibility of the implementation and is not visible to the user. The current compositing order may be set by calling *glVRCompositingOrderEXT* with one of the constants defined above. The default compositing order is GL_FRONT_TO_BACK_EXT.

```
GLvoid glVRCompositingOrderEXT
       (GLenum          order)
```

order   compositing order to be used

Once the fragment's color value has been determined, it is passed on to the "fragment operations" stages of the OpenGL pipeline for further processing. From this point on, the fragment is treated exactly the same as fragments generated by other OpenGL rendering pipelines.

FRAGMENT OPERATIONS

The fragment operations applied to fragments generated by the volume rendering pipeline are identical to those applied to fragments generated by the geometry pipeline and the pixel processing (imaging) pipeline. The fragment operations that are the most useful for volume rendering are blending and depth testing. If depth testing is enabled, each incoming fragment will have its depth value compared to the depth value stored in the depth buffer. If the test passes, the pixel value and the depth value will be replaced with the incoming fragment's color and depth value. This enables an application to merge transparent voxels with opaque geometry already rendered in the frame buffer.

The blending operation is similarly useful. If the blending equation is set to GL_MAX_EXT (as defined by the EXT_blend_minmax extension), only the maximum value for each color component will be written in the frame buffer. Similarly, if the blending equation is set to GL_MIN_EXT, only the minimum value will be written. The blending function can be set to its default value (GL_FUNC_ADD_EXT) to get the standard blending operations that take alpha into consideration, or to compute the sum of all of the incoming fragments.

ATTRIBUTE QUERIES

The following volume rendering attributes can be queried with the standard OpenGL *glGetBooleanv, glGetIntegerv, glGetFloatv*, and *glGetDoublev* calls:

GL_VR_OPTIMAL_BLOCK_WIDTH_EXT	Returns the width (in voxels) of the optimal block
GL_VR_OPTIMAL_BLOCK_HEIGHT_EXT	Returns the height (in voxels) of the optimal block
GL_VR_OPTIMAL_BLOCK_DEPTH_EXT	Returns the depth (in voxels) of the optimal block
GL_VR_BLOCK_WIDTH_EXT	Returns the width (in voxels) of the blocks in the current volume data set
GL_VR_BLOCK_HEIGHT_EXT	Returns the height (in voxels) of the blocks in the current volume data set
GL_VR_BLOCK_DEPTH_EXT	Returns the depth (in voxels) of the blocks in the current volume data set
GL_VR_VOLUME_WIDTH_EXT	Returns the width (in voxels) of the current volume data set

GL_VR_VOLUME_HEIGHT_EXT	Returns the height (in voxels) of the current volume data set
GL_VR_VOLUME_DEPTH_EXT	Returns the depth (in voxels) of the current volume data set
GL_VR_VOXEL_FORMAT_EXT	Returns the form of the voxels in the current volume data set
GL_VR_SCALE_X_EXT	Returns the scale factor for the X axis
GL_VR_SCALE_Y_EXT	Returns the scale factor for the Y axis
GL_VR_SCALE_Z_EXT	Returns the scale factor for the Z axis
GL_VR_INTENSITY_SHIFT_EXT	Returns the number of bits that the intensity value will be shifted
GL_VR_GRADIENT_MAGNITUDE_SHIFT_EXT	Returns the number of bits that the gradient magnitude value will be shifted
GL_VR_GRADIENT_MAGNITUDE_BITS_EXT	Returns the number of bits in the gradient magnitude
GL_VR_INDEX_SHIFT_EXT	Returns the number of bits that the index value will be shifted
GL_VR_MAX_LIGHTS_EXT	Returns the maximum number of light sources available for lighting voxels
GL_VR_SAMPLING_FREQUENCY_EXT	Returns the sampling frequency for the Z dimension
GL_VR_INTERP_METHOD_EXT	Returns the current interpolation method
GL_VR_COMPOSITING_ORDER_EXT	Returns the current compositing order

The following volume rendering attributes may be queried using the standard OpenGL *glIsEnabled* call:

GL_VR_VOXEL_MASK_TEST_EXT	Returns GL_TRUE if the voxel mask test is currently enabled
GL_VR_CLASSIFICATION_TABLE_EXT	Returns GL_TRUE if the classification table is currently enabled
GL_VR_COMPUTE_TABLE_INDEX_EXT	Returns GL_TRUE if the "compute table index" mode is currently enabled

The following volume rendering attributes may be queried using the standard OpenGL *glGetPointerv* call:

GL_VR_BLOCK_POINTERS_EXT	Returns a pointer to the array of block pointers for the current volume data set
GL_VR_BLOCK_ACTIONS_EXT	Returns a pointer to the array of block actions for the current volume data set
GL_VR_VOXEL_MASK_EXT	Returns a pointer to the array of block pointers that comprise the current voxel mask

UTILITIES

This section defines some utilities that can be used to create and manipulate volume data sets.

Slice-to-Block Conversion

Since many data sets are stored as a sequence of images (or slices), the API defines some utility functions to turn images into a volume data set with optimal blocking. Once this is done, the volume can be rendered as described above. The first step is to begin the definition of a volume data set by calling the following routine:

```
GLvoid gluVRNewVolumeEXT
        (GLsizei        width,
         GLsizei        height,
         GLenum         pixelformat,
         GLenum         pixeltype,
         GLenum         blocktype,
         GLenum         voxelformat)
```

width   width of each image (in pixels)
height   height of each image (in pixels)
pixelformat   format of pixels in each image (see *glDrawPixels*)
pixeltype   type of pixels in each image (see *glDrawPixels*)
blocktype   type of blocks to be generated
voxelformat   format of voxels to be generated (see *glVRVolume-DataEXT*)

The *width* and *height* parameters specify the size of the images that will be used to create the volume data set. The *pixelformat* and *pixeltype* arguments describe the organization of the pixels in each image and are identical to the *format* and *type* arguments to *gl-DrawPixels*. The *blocktype* argument indicates the type of blocks that will be generated. Permissible values are GL_VR_RENDER_UNCOMPRESSED_EXT and GL_VR_RENDER_COMPRESSED_EXT. The *voxelformat* argument defines the type of voxels that will be generated. The legal voxel formats are the same as those defined by the *glVRVolumeDataEXT* routine.

Once the definition of a new volume has begun, images are added to the data set by calling

```
GLvoid gluVRNextImageEXT
        (GLboolean      copyimage
         const GLvoid   *pixels)
```

copyimage   Boolean that indicates whether image data must be copied before returning

pixels   pointer to pixels that comprise the next slice

Applications should call the *gluVRNextImageEXT* to add each successive slice to the data set. If *copyimage* is GL_TRUE, the image data will be copied into the data set before the function returns. This allows the application to reuse the memory for the next slice. If *copyimage* is GL_FALSE, only the pointer to the pixels will be saved away. The application effectively guarantees that all of the slices will be in memory and the pointers will be valid at the time *gluVREndVolumeEXT* is called.

Once all the slices have been specified, the following routine is used to convert the slices into optimal blocks:

```
GLvoid gluVREndVolumeEXT
        (GLuint         *width,
         GLuint         *height,
         GLuint         *depth,
         GLuint         *numblocks,
         GLvoid**        *blockptrs)
```

width	returns the width (in voxels) of the generated volume data set
height	returns the height (in voxels) of the generated volume data set
depth	returns the depth (in voxels) of the generated volume data set
numblocks	returns the number of blocks that were generated
blockptrs	returns a pointer to an array containing pointers to the blocks

The values returned by *gluVREndVolumeEXT* describe the volume data set that was generated and can be passed directly to *glVRVolumeData* and its related routines in order to draw the volume. Blocks in the generated data set will be the width, height, and depth that are defined by the underlying implementation as the optimal block width, height, and depth. If the input image width, height, and number of slices are not even multiples of the optimal block width, height, and depth, the resulting volume data set will be padded by values containing all zeros. The generated volume data set (including the block pointer list and all of the blocks) can be deleted and the associated memory freed by calling:

```
GLvoid gluVRDeleteVolumeEXT
       (const GLvoid*     *blockptrs)
```

| *blockptrs* | Pointer to an array containing pointers to the blocks comprising a volume data set |

Converting Nonoptimal Blocks into Optimal Blocks

A volume data set might be organized into blocks that are not optimal for the underlying implementation. The following utility routine can be used to convert nonoptimal blocks to optimal blocks:

```
GLvoid gluVROptimizeBlocksEXT
       (GLuint        blkwidth,
        GLuint        blkheight,
        GLuint        blkdepth,
        GLuint        nblks,
```

```
const          GLvoid* *blkptrs,
GLuint          *newnblks
GLvoid**        *newblkptrs)
```

blkwidth   Width of blocks (in voxels) in original volume data set

blkheight   Height of blocks (in voxels) in original volume data set

blkdepth   Depth of blocks (in voxels) in original volume data set

nblks   Number of blocks in original volume data set

blkptrs   Pointer to an array containing pointers to the blocks comprising a volume data set

newnblks   Returns the number of blocks in the new volume data set

newblkptrs Returns a pointer to an array containing pointers to the blocks in the new volume data set

This routine converts the volume data set containing blocks of *blockwidth* x *blockheight* x *blockdepth* into a volume data set containing blocks of the optimal width, height, and depth. The generated volume data set and its associated memory may be destroyed by calling *gluVRDeleteVolumeEXT*.

Compress/Decompress Block

The following routines can be used to compress and decompress blocks in a volume data set:

```
GLvoid gluVRCompressBlockEXT
     (GLenum         format,
      const GLvoid   *original,
      GLvoid*        *converted)
```

format   format of the voxels in the original block

original   pointer to the voxels in the original block

converted   returns a pointer to the voxels in the compressed block

```
GLvoid gluVRDecompressBlockEXT
        (GLenum              format,
         const GLvoid        *original,
         GLvoid*             *converted)
```

format   format of the voxels in the original block
original   pointer to the voxels in the original block
converted   returns a pointer to the voxels in the decompressed
                block

The width, height, and depth of the block to be converted are obtained by querying the current OpenGL state. The format of the original block is specified by *format* and the block itself is referenced by *original*. A pointer to the converted block is returned in *converted*.

Extract Parallel Slice

The following utility routines can be used to extract a parallel slice from a volume data set and store the result into memory as an image:

```
GLvoid gluVRExtractXYImageEXT
        (GLuint              value,
         GLenum              pixelformat,
         GLenum              pixeltype,
         GLenum              blocktype,
         GLenum              voxelformat,
         const GLvoid*       *blockptrs)

GLvoid gluVRExtractXZImageEXT
        (GLuint              value,
         GLenum              pixelformat,
         GLenum              pixeltype,
         GLenum              blocktype,
         GLenum              voxelformat,
         const GLvoid*       *blockptrs)

GLvoid gluVRExtractYZImageEXT
        (GLuint              value,
```

```
GLenum        pixelformat,
GLenum        pixeltype,
GLenum        blocktype,
GLenum        voxelformat,
const GLvoid* *blockptrs)
```

value	number of the slice to be extracted
pixelformat	format of pixels in output image (see *glDrawPixels*)
pixeltype	type of pixels in output image (see *glDrawPixels*)
blocktype	type of blocks in volume data set
voxelformat	format of voxels in volume data set (see *glVRVolumeDataEXT*)
blockptrs	Pointer to an array containing pointers to the blocks comprising a volume data set

These three utilities operate in a similar fashion. Depending on the routine called, an image is extracted from the volume data set parallel to the *XY* plane, the *XZ* plane, or the *YZ* plane. The value argument specifies the distance (in voxels) from the target plane. The *pixelformat* and *pixeltype* arguments describe the organization of the pixels in each image and are identical to the *format* and *type* arguments to *glDrawPixels*. The *blocktype* argument indicates the type of blocks in the volume data set. Permissible values are GL_VR_RENDER_UNCOMPRESSED_EXT and GL_VR_RENDER_COMPRESSED_EXT. The *voxelformat* argument defines the type of voxels in the volume data set. The legal voxel formats are the same as those defined by the *glVRVolumeDataEXT* routine.

USAGE NOTES

Drawing Volumes and Opaque Geometry

OpenGL requires applications to sort transparent geometry in depth order and render from front-to-back to achieve transparency effects. This is because OpenGL is inherently immediate mode—there is no intermediate storage in which objects can be collected and sorted prior to rendering.

Volume data sets are usually rendered with nonopaque voxels. In order to mix opaque geometry and volumes and achieve the desired results, applications must first render all of the opaque geometry in the scene. Once the opaque geometry has been rendered, the volume data set can be rendered, and if the OpenGL fragment operations have been set up properly, transparent voxels will be rendered properly. If depth testing is enabled, voxels that are behind opaque geometry will not be rendered, while those in front of opaque geometry can be properly blended.

Drawing Volumes and Transparent Geometry

Transparent geometry that is either completely in front of the volume or completely behind the volume can also be rendered properly. All transparent objects, including the volume, must be drawn in front-to-back order. It is not currently possible to properly render multiple overlapping transparent objects, unless they are first divided into nonoverlapping objects.

FUTURES

Data Formats

The following voxel data formats have received some consideration. We could consider supporting any or all of these as an extension beyond the basic capabilities. We would also consider adding other formats that could be shown to be generally useful.

- GL_RGB565_EXT (Q: How is opacity determined? A: It is assumed to be 1.0)
- GL_RGB332_EXT (Q: How is opacity determined? A: It is assumed to be 1.0)
- GL_INTENSITY16_INDEX8_XYZ888_EXT (We're deferring all formats greater than 32 bits)
- GL_RGBA8888_INTENSITY8_XYZ888_EXT (Potential feedback result, but greater than 32 bits)

Gradient Computation Methods

It is possible that some vendors will want to support a gradient computation method other than central differences. This is left to a future (or vendor-specific) extension.

Boundary Wrap Modes

It is possible that some vendors will want to support boundary wrap modes other than the reduction mode that is currently defined. This is left to a future (or vendor-specific) extension.

Interpolation Modes

It is possible that some vendors will want to support an interpolation method that is of higher order than GL_LINEAR. This is left to a future (or vendor-specific) extension.

Feedback

There have been requests for a feedback mechanism in the voxel pipeline. One use of this would be to compute gradients in the first pass and then supply voxel values with gradients to avoid the unnecessary computation of gradients each subsequent time the data set is rendered. It may also be the case that applications need a mechanism for performing some analysis on the final color value of each voxel. Our thought is that such a feedback "tap" would occur right after the lighting stage of the voxel pipeline, so that both color and normal values could be returned. There are a number of issues with defining such a feedback mechanism in hardware, so it may be the case that this type of feedback mechanism would always be implemented in software. And if this is the case, the same things could be accomplished with utilities. If a compelling case can be built for including a feedback stage in the voxel pipeline, we are open to including it.

Rendering Multiple Overlapping Volumes

Several organizations have expressed the need to render multiple overlapping volumes. The API does not currently support the proper rendering of multiple overlapping volumes, since it requires applications to draw one volume first, and then the other. There is no mechanism for defining several volumes and rendering them simultaneously.

This limitation could be overcome by adding *glVRBeginMultiVolumeEXT* and *glVREndMultiVolumeEXT* calls. These calls would serve to bracket a sequence of calls to *glVRDrawVolumeEXT* that would define the volume data sets to be rendered. The volume data sets would then be processed simultaneously when *glVREndMultiVolumeEXT* was called.

However, there are still a number of issues that would need to be resolved. We would need some mechanism for describing the blending behavior at sample points where there are contributions from voxels from more than one data set. We would also need to decide which state attributes could be modified within the begin/end pair (e.g., could lighting and material properties be changed?). There have been discussions of adding BeginFrame/EndFrame calls to OpenGL. Since these would provide more general semantics, it might be reasonable to make use of them rather than the specific begin/end proposed here.

The current solution to the rendering of multiple overlapping volumes is for applications to combine multiple volumes into a single volume and then render the result with *glVRDrawVolumeEXT*.

Transparent Geometry within a Volume

As noted above, it is possible to mix opaque geometry and volumes, even if the geometry is within a volume. It is also possible to render transparent geometry that is completely outside of a volume. The application must sort the geometry and volume(s) in depth order and render things from front to back.

Transparent geometry within a volume cannot be drawn correctly at this time, since the API requires you to either draw the geometry first or the volume first. Unless the application rasterizes the geometry into the volume data set directly, there is no way to achieve a totally correct rendering.

This issue could be resolved with the addition of the support for rendering multiple volume data sets as described above. Transparent geometry within a volume data set could be rendered properly if geometry calls were permitted within the *glVRBeginMultiVolumeEXT/glVREndMultiVolumeEXT* pair. Geometry calls and calls to *glVRDrawVolumeEXT* that occur between the begin/end pair would be buffered and would all be processed simultaneously when the call to *glVREndMultiVolumeEXT* occurred. Geometry would be rasterized into a volume data set, and all the volume data sets would be combined into a single, simultaneous rendering.

The current solution to properly render transparent geometry within a volume is to split the volume into two parts, draw the part of the volume in front of the geometry first, then draw the geometry, and then draw the part of the volume behind the geometry.

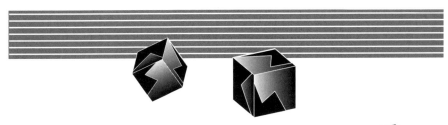

GLOSSARY

Achromatic The absence of color. Something that is achromatic is in the range from black through gray to white.

Adaptive algorithm An algorithm that processes data without any prior knowledge of its nature. As data is processed, the algorithm adapts. Examples of adaptive algorithms include adaptive filters and adaptive encoders.

Affine transformation A linear geometric transformation that includes rotation, translation, scaling, shear, and any combination of them.

Algorithm A set of steps used to solve a problem or perform an operation.

Aliasing A result of sampling an image at a rate less than twice the highest spatial frequency in the image. Aliasing in an image can manifest itself as jagged stair casing along the edges of diagonal lines.

Alpha channel Storage for values used in alpha blending. These control values are known as alphas. Alpha blending provides a means of creating a new pixel by combining portions of two existing pixels. Data in the alpha channel sets the translucency of an object.

Bilinear interpolation A method of creating a new value between four known values. The process involves linear interpolation in two directions.

Brightness The attribute of visual perception in which a source emits a degree of light. This differs from lightness in that brightness refers to self-luminous objects.

CAT Computer-aided tomography. See CT.

CT Computed tomography. This is an image acquisition system that uses X-rays. It is typically used to acquire skeletal images.

Classification The process of determining what set of values to make visible. This is done by assigning opacities.

Compositing The process of combining portions of several images into one image.

Compression This is a process used to represent data with less data. This can be done by removing redundant information. Another technique is to represent the most frequently occurring datum in a data stream with a shorter datum.

Contrast The variation in brightness between the darkest and lightest regions of an image.

Contrast stretching A technique used to increase the contrast in a low-contrast image.

Convolution An image operation used for such effects as smoothing and sharpening. The process is fairly simple. A weighted sum of the pixels in the neighborhood of the source pixel is placed in the same location (row and column) of the source pixel. The weights are organized in an array called the convolution kernel or mask.

Convolution coefficient An individual weight in a convolution kernel or mask.

Convolution kernel The array of convolution coefficients. It is also called a convolution mask.

Convolution mask The array of convolution coefficients. It is also called a convolution kernel.

Cubic Spline A function that is used as an interpolation kernel. Though it is compute intensive, it yields superior quality interpolations.

Digitization The process of transforming a continuous image into digital data. This requires sampling and quantizing.

Filter Device or technique to remove specific components of a signal. In its purest form, a filter removes specific components of an image. In some cases, this is the high- or low-spatial frequency data.

Finite impulse response filters (FIR)   Nonrecursive digital filters that have outputs dependent on current and previous inputs.

Frame buffer   The memory in a graphics system that stores the data shown on the display. If using double-buffered graphics, the display toggles between two frame buffers. This is used in animation to display one frame buffer while creating the next frame in the second frame buffer.

Frequency domain   A representation of a signal according to its basic frequency components.

Frequency transform   This is an operation that converts an image into a representation of fundamental frequency components.

Gamma   The nonlinear characteristics of imaging devices. In a nonlinear display, a small change in the brightness when the level is low is not the same magnitude as the same size change when the level is high.

Gray scale   The range of shades from black to white. Gray scale is typically but not limited to 256 levels.

High-pass filter   A digital filter which allows high spatial frequencies (fine detail) to pass while attenuating the low-spatial frequencies.

Histogram   A bar-graph representation of the frequency of pixel intensities in an image.

Histogram equalization   A technique used to uniformly distribute the pixel values of an image to fill the entire possible dynamic range.

Hole   Holes, also called patches, are the results of pixels without mapped input values. They are an artifact of forward projections.

Hue   This is what is popularly referred to as color. Technically, hue corresponds to the wavelength of the color.

Intensity   Amplitude or power of light.

Interpolation   A class of techniques used to generate missing data between known surrounding points. Bilinear interpolation, for example, assumes a linear relationship between the points known.

Jaggies   The stair casing of diagonal edges in an image. It can be a product of aliasing.

Lightness   The intensity of nonself-luminous objects.

Look-up table (LUT)   A table of values in which the index to the table represents the value it points to.

Lossless encoding   Data compression in which no information is lost in the compression stage. If an image is compressed and decompressed with a lossless algorithm, the decompressed image will be identical to the original image.

Lossy encoding   Data compression in which information was lost in the compression stage. This lost information cannot be recovered. The differences between the original image and the compressed and decompressed image may or may not be noticeable. Typically, the more information that is lost during lossy compression, the greater the compression ratio. There is a trade-off between image quality and compression ratios.

Low-pass filter   A digital filter that passes the low spatial frequencies and attenuates the high frequencies. These filters smooth or blur an image.

Luminance   The intensity or brightness of a pixel.

MRI   Magnetic resonance imaging. A tomographic image system that can gather cross-section slice images.

MSI   Magnetic source imaging. An image system that monitors the electric signals in the brain during thinking and motor functions.

Magnification   The operation of enlarging an image.

Marching cubes   This method of volume rendering consists of finding edge orientation in data sets and rendering surfaces at these edges.

Monochrome   Consisting of one color. This term has been used to describe black and white images and the old green (or orange) graphics displays.

Nearest neighbor interpolation   A simple interpolation technique that uses the nearest existing sample value as the interpolated value.

Noise   A random variation in signal value occurring during digitizing, transmission, or other processes in a digital system.

Nyquist criterion   A restriction that requires a signal be sampled at a rate greater than twice that of its highest frequency component. During image acquisition (or any data acquisition), if this requirement is not met, aliasing is a result.

Opacity   A value assigned to a voxel to represent "transparency." The process of assigning opacities, classification, determines what part of the data set should be visible and which should not.

PET   Positron emission tomography. A tomographic image system is used to gather cross-sectional image data. It is used primarily to monitor the body's chemical processes.

Palette This is a set of colors selected from the full gamut that a nontrue color graphics system can display. This is the look-up table portion of a colormap.

Perspective projection A geometric transformation also called projective mapping. It is a projection from one plane through a point onto another plane.

Pixel A picture element. An image is composed of many tiny dots. These dots are pixels.

Primary colors A small set of colors which can be combined in various proportions to reproduce all other colors. In additive color systems, these colors are red, green, and blue.

Pseudo color A color mapping of achromatic data. This is done with temperature profiles. In an image, the colder temperatures are represented as shades of blue. The higher temperatures are represented with shades of red.

Quantization The process of determining the digital value of an analog signal.

Quantization error The error introduced when a continuous signal is represented with a limited number of levels, which results in reduced precision. The error is the difference between the original signal and its representation.

Raster A set of scan lines that make up a computer display or a TV picture. Raster graphics refers to an image composed of an array of pixels arranged in rows and columns.

Ray casting A method of volume rendering. It involves passing rays through a three-dimensional data set compositing samples along each ray. The end product is a two-dimensional image.

Reflectance The portion of incident light that is reflected off an object.

Resampling Sampling already sampled data at a different sample rate. This can include scaling an image up or down.

Resolution A measure of image samples. Printers define this in dots per inch (dpi). This term is also used loosely as an image's dimensions.

RGB The additive color space consisting of the primaries red, green, and blue. This color model is used in most computer graphics display hardware.

Sampling The chopping of an analog video signal into discrete pixels. In its purest definition, this process does not include quantization.

Scaling   The process that enlarges or shrinks an image.

Scan line   One line or row of an image or a display.

Scientific visualization   A field of study that graphically represents data that is not directly observable.

Separability   The property that allows a multidimensional operation to be resolved into several one-dimensional operations. This is advantageous from a computational point of view.

Shading   This operation alters voxel values dependent on their location with reference to the light source.

Sharpening   An image operation, based on high-pass filtering, that increases the visual sharpness of an image.

Spatial frequency   Characterization of cyclical properties in an image. Intensity fluctuations occurring in close proximity are considered high spatial frequencies. Regions of constant intensity or slowly varying intensity are low spatial frequencies.

Spatial domain   The normal domain of image data: intensity as a function of position.

Splatting   This method of volume rendering involves projecting each voxel onto the screen. As it "splats" on the screen, its influence is felt by a neighboring group of pixels. The intensity of that voxel is shared accordingly.

Ultrasound   A mode for sampling acoustical impedance. It is based on emitting high-frequency pulses into an object and monitoring the returning echos.

Visual acuity   The degree to which two separate objects can be distinguished from each other.

Volume rendering   The technique used to display a three-dimensional model of captured image data.

Voxel   A three-dimensional sample.

Windowing function   A function applied to image data before applying the Fourier transform. It reduces the image edge discontinuities resulting from the Fourier transform's periodic interpretation of functions.

Zoom   Zoom is the act of magnifying an image or a portion of the image.

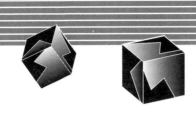

REFERENCES

1. R. Avila, T. He, L. Hong, A. Kaufman, H. Pfister, C. Silva, L. Sobierajski, and S. Wang. VolVis: A Diversified Volume Visualization System. In *Proceedings IEEE Visualization 1994*. IEEE Computer Society Press, 1994.

2. K. Akeley and T. Jermoluk. High-Performance Polygon Rendering. *Computer Graphics,* 22(4):239–246, August 1988.

3. K. Akeley. Reality Engine Graphics. In *Proceedings of SIGGRAPH 93,* pp. 109–116. ACM SIGGRAPH, New York, 1993.

4. L. Adams, W. Krybus, D. Meyer-Ebrecht, R. Ruger, J.M. Gilsbach, R. Moesges, and G. Schloendorff. Computer-Assisted Surgery. *IEEE Computer Graphics and Applications,* pp. 43–51, May 1990.

5. A.A. Apodace and M.W. Mantle. RenderMan: Pursuing the Future of Graphics. *IEEE Computer Graphics and Applications,* 10(4):44–49, July 1990.

6. J. Amanatides. Realism in Computer Graphics: A Survey. *IEEE Computer Graphics and Applications,* 7(1):44–56, January 1987.

7. C. Barillot. Surface and Volume Rendering Techniques to Display 3D Data. *IEEE Engineering in Medicine and Biology,* 12(1):111–119, March 1993.

8. M.J. Bentum, M.A. Boer, A.G.J. Nijmeijer, M.M. Samsom, and C.H. Slump. Resampling of Images in Real-Time. In *Proceedings of the IEEE ProRISC Workshop on Circuit, Systems and Signal Processing,* pp. 21–26, 1994.

9. N. Binenbaum, L. Dias, C.H. Ju, S. Markel, J.C. Pearson, and H. Taylor. Neural Networks for Signal/Image Processing using the Princeton Engine Multi-Processor. In *IEEE Workshop on Signal Processing and Neural Nets,* pp. 595–605, 1991.

10. M.J. Bentum. *Interactive Visualization of Volume Data.* Ph.D. thesis, University of Twente, December 1995.

11. L. Bergman, H. Fuchs, E. Grant, and S. Spach. Image Rendering by Adaptive Refinement. *Computer Graphics*, 20(4):29–35, August 1986.

12. M. Bomans, K.H. Hoehne, U. Tiede, and M. Riemer. 3-D Segmentation of MR Images of the Head for 3-D Display. *IEEE Transactions on Medical Imaging*, 9(2):177–183, June 1990.

13. R. Bakalash, A. Kaufman, R. Pacheco, and H. Pfister. An Extended Volume Visualization System for Arbitrary Parallel Projection. In *Proceedings of the Seventh Workshop on Graphics Hardware*, Vol. EG92 HW, pp. 64–69. EuroGraphics Technical Report Series, 1992.

14. S. Bright and S. Laflin. Shading of Solid Voxel Models. *Computer Graphics Forum*, 5(2):131–137, June 1986.

15. J.F. Blinn. Light Reflection Functions for Simulation of Clouds and Dusty Surfaces. *Computer Graphics*, 16(3):21–29, July 1982.

16. J. Blinn. Jim Blinn's Corner: Compositing, Part I: Theory, *IEEE Computer Graphics and Applications*, pp. 83–87, September 1994.

17. M.J. Bentum, B.B.A. Lichtenbelt, and T. Malzbender. Analysis of Gradient Estimators in Volume Rendering. *IEEE Transactions on Visualization and Computer Graphics*, 2(3):242–254, September 1996.

18. OpenGL Architecture Review Board. *OpenGL Programming Guide*. Addison-Wesley Developers Press, 2nd ed., 1997.

19. OpenGL Architecture Review Board. *OpenGL Reference Manual*. Addison-Wesley Developers Press, 2nd ed., 1997.

20. Paul A. Bottomley. Nuclear Magnetic Resonance: Beyond Physical Imaging. *IEEE Spectrum*, pp. 32–38, February 1983.

21. R.N. Bracewell. *The Fourier Transform and Its Applications*. McGraw-Hill, 1986.

22. M.J. Bentum and J. Smit. Design of a Parallel VLSI Engine for Real-Time Visualization of 3D Medical Images. In *Proceedings of SPIE Medical Imaging 1994*, Vol. 2164, pp. 370–381. SPIE—The International Society for Optical Engineering, 1994.

23. M. Bosma, J. Smit, and J. Terwisscha van Scheltinga. Super Resolution Volume Rendering Hardware. In *Proceedings of the Tenth Workshop on Graphics Hardware*, Vol. EG95 HW. EuroGraphics Technical Report Series, ISSN 1024–0861, Maastricht, The Netherlands, August 1995.

24. L.J. Brewster, S.S. Trivedi, H.K. Tuy, and J.K. Udupa. Interactive Surgical Planning. *IEEE Computer Graphics and Applications*, 4(3):31–40, March 1984.

25. M. Bosma and J. Terwisscha van Scheltinga. Efficient Super Resolution Volume Rendering. Master's thesis, University of Twente, August 1995.

26. M. Born and E. Wolf. *Principles of Optics: Electromagnetic Theory of Propagation, Interference, and Diffraction of Light*. Pergamon Press, 1975.

27. I. Carlbom. Optimal Filter Design for Volume Reconstruction. In *Proceedings IEEE Visualization 1993*, pp. 54–61. IEEE Computer Society Press, October 1993.

28. B. Cabral, N. Cam, and J. Foran. Accelerated Volume Rendering and Tomographic Reconstruction Using Texture Mapping Hardware. *IEEE/ACM Symposium on Volume Visualization*, pp. 91–98, October 1994.

29. L. Chang, H. Chen, and J. Ro. Reconstruction of 3D Medical Images: A Nonlinear Interpolation Technique for Reconstruction of 3D Medical Images. *Computer Vision, Graphics and Image Processing: Graphical Models and Image Processing,* 53(4):382–391, July 1991.

30. T. Chiueh. A Novel Memory Access Mechanism for Arbitrary-View-Projection Volume Rendering. Technical Report, State University of New York at Stony Brook, 1993.

31. T. Chiueh, T. He, A. Kaufman, and H. Pfister. Compression Domain Volume Rendering. Technical Report, State University of New York at Stony Brook, 1994.

32. L. Chen, G.T. Herman, R.A. Reynolds, and J.K. Udupa. Surface Shading in the Cuberille Environment. *IEEE Computer Graphics and Application,* 5(12):33–43, December 1985.

33. D. Cohen, A. Kaufman, R. Bakalash, and S. Bergman. Real Time Discrete Shading. *The Visual Computer,* 6(1):16–27, February 1990.

34. H.E. Cline, W.E. Lorendsen, S. Ludke, C.R. Crawford, and B.C. Teeter. Two Algorithms for 3-D Reconstruction of Tomograms. *Medical Physics,* 15(3):320–327, May/June 1988.

35. S. Chen, W. Lin, C. Liang, and C. Chen. Improvement on Dynamic Elastic Interpolation Technique for Reconstructing 3D Objects from Serial Cross Sections. *IEEE Transactions on Medical Imaging,* 9(1):71–83, March 1990.

36. T.J. Cullip and U. Neumann. Accelerating Volume Reconstruction with 3D Texture Hardware. Technical report, University of North Carolina at Chapel Hill, 1993.

37. P.C. Come. *Diagnostic Cardiology, Noninvasive Imaging Techniques.* J.B. Lippincott Company, 1985.

38. D. Chin, J. Passe, F. Bernard, H. Taylor, and S. Knights. The Princeton Engine: A Real-Time Video System Simulator. *IEEE Transactions on Consumer Electronics,* 34(2):285–297, May 1988.

39. M.F. Cohen, J. Painter, M. Mehta, and Kwan-Liu Ma. Volume Seedlings. *ACM Symposium on Interactive 3D Graphics,* pp. 139–145, March/April 1992.

40. E. Catmull and R. Rom. *Computer Aided Geometric Design.* Academic Press, 1974.

41. J.L. Coatrieux, C. Toumoulin, C. Hamon, and L. Luo. Future Trends in 3D Medical Imaging. *IEEE Engineering in Medicine and Biology,* 9(4):33–39, December 1990.

42. M. de Boer, J. Hesser, A. Gropt, T. Gunther, C. Poliwoda, C. Reinhart, and R. Manner. Evaluation of a Real-Time Direct Volume Rendering System. In *Proceedings of the 11th Workshop on Graphics Hardware,* Vol. EG96 HW, pp. 109–119. EuroGraphics Technical Report Series, Poitiers, France, August 1996.

43. R.A. Drebin, L. Carpenter, and P. Hanrahan. Volume Rendering. *Computer Graphics,* 22(4):65–74, August 1988.

44. R.O. Duda and P.E. Hart. In *Pattern Classification and Scene Analysis,* pp. 271–272. John Wiley and Sons, New York, 1973.

45. M.C. Doggett and G.R. Hellestrand. A Hardware Architecture for Video Rate Smooth Shading of Volume Data. In *Proceedings Ninth Eurographics*

Workshop on Graphics Hardware, Vol. EG94 HW, pp. 95–102. EuroGraphics Technical Report Series ISSN 1017-4656, 1994.

46. W. Strasser and D. Jackel. Reconstructing Solids from Tomographic Scans— The Parcum-II System. In A.A.M. Kuijk and W. Strasser, eds. *Advances in Computer Graphics Hardware II,* pp. 209–227. Springer-Verlag ISBN 0-387-50109-6, 1988.

47. S. Dunne, S. Napel, and B. Rutt. Fast Reprojection of Volume Data. *Proceedings of the 1st Conference on Visualization in Biomedical Computing,* 11–18, IEEE CS Press, May 1990, ISBN 0-818-62039-0.

48. M. Doggett. An Array Based Design for Real-Time Volume Rendering. In *Proceedings of the Tenth Workshop on Graphics Hardware,* Vol. EG95 HW, pp. 93–101. EuroGraphics Technical Report Series, ISSN 1024–0861, Maastricht, The Netherlands, August 1995.

49. R.A. Drebin. Volumetric Rendering of Computed Tomography Data: Principles and Techniques. *IEEE Computer Graphics and Applications,* 10(2): 24–32, March 1990.

50. S. Dellepiane, S.B. Serpico, and G. Vernazza. A Framework for Processing and Interpretation of Three-Dimensional Signals from Multislices. *Signal Processing,* 18(3):239–258, November 1989.

51. D. Dudgeon. *Multidimensional Signal Processing.* Prentice Hall, 1984.

52. R. Duncan. A Survey of Parallel Computer Architectures. *IEEE Computer,* 23(2):5–16, February 1990.

53. J. Eyles, J. Austin, H. Fuchs, T. Greer, and J. Poulton. Pixel-Planes 4: A Summary. In *Advances in Computer Graphics Hardware II,* pp. 183–208. Springer-Verlag, 1988.

54. T.T. Elvins. A Survey of Algorithms for Volume Visualization. *Computer Graphics,* 26(3):194–201, August 1992.

55. G. Frieder, D. Gordon, and R.A. Reynolds. Back-to-Front Display of Voxel-Based Objects. *IEEE Computer Graphics and Application,* 5(1):52–60, January 1985.

56. G. Frieder, G.T. Herman, C. Meyer, and J. Udupa. Large Software Problems for Small Computers: An Example from Medical Imaging. *IEEE Software,* 2(5):37–47, September 1985.

57. E. Fiume. A Mathematical Semantics of Rendering I: Ideal Rendering. *Computer Vision, Graphics and Image Processing,* 48(3):281–303, December 1989.

58. E. Fiume. A Mathematical Semantics of Rendering II: Approximation. *Computer Vision, Graphics and Image Processing,* 53(1):19–34, January 1991.

59. B. Friedman, J.P. Jones, G. Chaves-Munoz, A.P. Salmon, and C.R.B. Merritt. *Principles of MRI.* McGraw-Hill, 1989.

60. H. Fuchs, Z.M. Kedam, and S.P. Uselton. Optimal Surface Reconstruction from Planar Contours. *Communications of the ACM,* 20(10):693–702, October 1977.

61. H. Fuchs, M.S. Levoy, and S. Pizer. Interactive Visualization of 3D Medical Data. *Computer,* pp. 46–50, August 1989.

62. H. Fuchs, J. Poulton, J. Eyles, T. Greer, J. Goldfeather, D. Ellsworth, S. Molnar, G. Turk, B. Tebbs, and L. Israel. Pixel-Planes 5: A Heterogeneous Multi-

processor Graphics System Using Processor-Enhanced Memories. *Computer Graphics,* 23(3):79–88, July 1989.

63. K.A. Frenkel. Volume Rendering. *Communications of the ACM,* 32(4):426–435, April 1989.

64. J.D. Foley and A. van Dam. *Fundamentals of Interactive Computer Graphics.* Addison-Wesley, 1984.

65. J.D. Foley, A. van Dam, S.K. Feiner, and J.F. Hughes. *Computer Graphics: Principles and Practice, 2nd ed.* Addison-Wesley, 1990.

66. E.J. Farrell, W.C. Yang, and R.A. Zappulla. Animated 3D CT Imaging. *IEEE Computer Graphics and Applications,* 5(12): 26–32, December 1985.

67. M.P. Garrity. Raytracing Irregular Volume Data. *Computer Graphics,* 24(5):35–40, November 1990.

68. C. Giertsen. Volume Visualization of Sparse Irregular Meshes. *IEEE Computer Graphics and Applications,* pp. 40–48, March 1992.

69. W. Strasser and G. Knittel. A Compact Volume Rendering Accelerator. *IEEE/ACM Symposium on Volume Visualization,* pp. 67–94, October 1994.

70. A. Van Gelder and K. Kim. Direct Volume Rendering with Shading via Three-Dimensional Textures. *IEEE Symposium on Volume Visualization,* pp. 23–28, October 1996.

71. S.Y. Guan and R. Lipes. Innovative Volume Rendering using 3D Texture Mapping. In *Proceedings of SPIE Medical Imaging 1994,* Vol. 2164, pp. 382–392. SPIE—The International Society for Optical Engineering, 1994.

72. A.S. Glassner. Ray Tracing for Realism. *Byte,* pp. 263–271, December 1990.

73. M.A. Gehring, T.R. Mackie, S.S. Kubsad, B.P. Paliwal, M.P. Mehta, and T.J. Kinsella. A Three-Dimensional Volume Visualization Package applied to Stereotactic Radiosurgery Treatment Planning. *Int. J. Radiation Oncology Biology Physics,* 21(2):491–500, July 1991.

74. D.S. Goodsell, I.S. Mian, and A.J. Olson. Rendering Volumetric Data in Molecular Systems. *Journal of Molecular Graphics,* 7:35–36, 41–47, March 1989.

75. S.M. Goldwasser. A generalized object display processor architecture. *IEEE Computer Graphics Applications,* 4(10):43–55, October 1984.

76. M.E. Goss. An Adjustable Gradient Filter for Volume Visualization Image Enhancement. In *Proceedings Graphics Interface '94,* pp. 67–74. Canadian Inf. Process. Soc., Toronto, Ont., Canada, 1994.

77. H. Gouraud. Continuous Shading of Curved Surfaces. *IEEE Transactions on Computers,* 20(6):623–629, 1971.

78. T. Gunther, C. Poliwoda, C. Reinhart, J. Hesser, R. Manner, H.P. Meinzer, and H.J. Baur. VIRIM: A Massively Parallel Processor for Real-Time Volume Visualization in Medicine. In *Proceedings Ninth Eurographics Workshop on Graphics Hardware,* Vol. EG94 HW, pp. 103–108. EuroGraphics Technical Report Series ISSN 1017–4656, 1994.

79. D. Gordon and R.A. Reynolds. Image Space Shading of 3-Dimensional Objects. *Computer Vision, Graphics and Image Processing,* 29:361–376, 1985.

80. S.M. Goldwasser and R.A. Reynolds. Real-Time Display and Manipulation of 3D Medical Objects: The Voxel Processor Architecture. *Computer Vision, Graphics and Image Processing,* 39:1–27, 1987.

81. B. Gudmundsson and M. Randen. Compression of Sequences of 3D Volume Surface Projections. *Proceedings Information Processing in Medical Imaging 1991,* pp. 501–510, 1991.

82. S.M. Goldwasser, R.A. Reynolds, T. Bapty, D. Baraff, J. Summers, D.A. Talton, and E. Walsch. A Physician's Workstation with Real-Time Performance. *IEEE Computer Graphics and Applications,* 44–57, December 1985.

83. S.M. Goldwasser, R.A. Reynolds, D.A. Dalton, and E.S. Walsch. Techniques for the Rapid Display and Manipulations of 3D Biomedical Data. *Computed Medical Imaging and Graphics,* 12(1):1–24, 1988.

84. G.J. Grevera and J.K. Udupa. Shape-Based Interpolation of Multidimensional Gray-Level Images. In *Proceedings SPIE-MI94,* Vol. 2164, pp. 14–21. SPIE, 1994.

85. A. Van Gelder and J. Wilhelms. Rapid Exploration of Curvilinear Grids Using Direct Volume Rendering (Extended Abstract). In *Proceedings IEEE Visualization 1993,* pp. 70–77. IEEE Computer Society Press, October 1993.

86. H.S. Hou and H.C. Andrews. Cubic Splines for Image Interpolation and Digital Filtering. *IEEE Transactions on Acoustics, Speech, and Signal Processing,* ASSP-26(6):508–517, December 1978.

87. P. Hanrahan. Three-Pass Affine Transform for Volume Rendering. *Computer Graphics,* 24(5):71–78, November 1990.

88. K.H. Hoehne and R. Bernstein. Shading 3D Images from CT Using Gray-Level Gradients. *IEEE Transactions on Medical Imaging,* 5(1):45–47, March 1986.

89. K.H. Hoehne, M. Bomans, A. Pommert, M. Riemer, C. Shiers, U. Tiede, and G. Wiebecke. 3D Visualization of Tomographic Volume Data Using the Generalized Voxel Model. *The Visual Computer,* 6(1):28–36, February 1990.

90. K.H. Hoehne, M. Bomans, M. Riemer, R. Schubert, U. Tiede, and W. Lierse. A Volume-based Anatomical Atlas. *IEEE Computer Graphics and Applications,* 12(4):72–78, July 1992.

91. B.M. Hemminger, T.J. Cullip, and M.J. North. Interactive Visualization of 3D Medical Image Data. Technical Report, University of North Carolina, Chapel Hill, Department of Computer Science, 1994.

92. G.T. Herman. *Image Reconstruction from Projections: The Fundamentals of Computerized Tomography.* Academic Press, 1980.

93. G.T. Herman. A Survey of 3D Medical Imaging Technologies. *IEEE Engineering in Medicine and Biology,* pp. 15–17, December 1990.

94. K. Hinckley, J.C. Goble, R. Pausch, and N.F. Kasell. New Applications for the Touchscreens in 2D and 3D Medical Imaging Workstations. In *Proceedings of SPIE Medical Imaging 1995,* Vol. 2431. SPIE—The International Society for Optical Engineering, 1995.

95. T. He, L. Hong, A. Kaufman, and H. Pfister. Generation of Transfer Functions with Stochastic Search Techniques. In *Proceedings IEEE Visualization 1996,* pp. 227–234. IEEE Computer Society Press, October 1996.

96. T. He and A.E. Kaufman. Virtual Input Devices for 3D Systems. In *Proceedings IEEE Visualization 1993,* pp. 142–148. IEEE Computer Society Press, 1993.

97. T. He and A.E. Kaufman. Virtual Input Devices for a Virtual World. In *Proceedings Virtual Reality Systems 1993*, IEEE CS Press, October 1993.

98. T. He and A. Kaufman. Nonexistence of the Wavelet Slice-Projection Theorem. Technical Report, State University of New York at Stony Brook, October 1994.

99. G.T. Herman and H.K. Liu. Three-Dimensional Display of Human Organs from Computed Tomograms. *Computer Graphics and Image Processing*, pp. 1–21, January 1979.

100. W.S. Hinshaw and A.H. Lent. An Introduction to NMR Imaging: From the Block Equation to the Imaging Equation. *Proceedings of the IEEE*, 71(3):338–350, March 1983.

101. B.M. Hemminger, P.L. Molina, P.M. Braeuning, F.C. Detterbeck, T.M. Egan, E.D. Pisano, and D.V. Beard. Clinical Applications of Real-Time Volume Rendering. In *Proceedings of SPIE Medical Imaging 1995*, Vol. 2431. SPIE—The International Society for Optical Engineering, 1995.

102. G.T. Herman and D. Odher. Visualizing Optimization by Multiple Processors. *IEEE Computer Graphics and Applications*, pp. 13–15, November 1991.

103. W. Hibbard and D. Santek. Visualizing Large Data Sets in the Earth Sciences. *Computer*, pp. 53–57, August 1989.

104. G.T. Herman and J.K. Udupa. Display of 3-D Objects: Computational Foundations and Medical Applications. *IEEE Computer Graphics and Applications*, pp. 39–46, August 1983.

105. S. Juskiw, N.G. Durdle, V.J. Raso, and D.L. Hill. Interactive Rendering of Volumetric Data Sets. In *Proceedings 9th Eurographics Workshop on Graphics Hardware*, Vol. EG94 HW, pp. 86–94. EuroGraphics Technical Report Series ISSN 1017–4656, 1994.

106. G.J. Jense. *Interactive Inspection of Volume Data*. Ph.D. thesis, University of Leiden, June 1991.

107. J.M. Jong, H.W. Park, K.S. Eo, M.H. Kim, P. Zhang, and Y. Kim. UWGSP4: An Imaging and Graphics Superworkstation and Its Medical Applications. In *Proceedings SPIE Medical Imaging VI*, Vol. 1653. SPIE, 1992.

108. J.T. Kajiya. Ray Tracing Volume Densities. *Computer Graphics*, (3):165–174, July 1984.

109. J.T. Kajiya. The Rendering Equation. *Computer Graphics*, 20(4):143–150, August 1986.

110. A. Kaufman. Efficient Algorithms for 3D Scan-Conversion of Parametric Curves, Surfaces, and Volumes. *Computer Graphics*, 21(4):171–179, July 1987.

111. A. Kaufman. Efficient Algorithms for Scan-Converting 3D Polygons. *Computers and Graphics*, 12(2):213–219, 1988.

112. A. Kaufman. *Volume Visualization*. IEEE Computer Society Press Tutorial, Los Alamitos, CA, 1991.

113. A. Kaufman and R. Bakalash. Memory and Processing Architectures for 3D Voxel-Based Imagery. *IEEE Computer Graphics and Applications*, 8(6): 10–23, November 1988.

114. A. Kaufman, R. Bakalash, D. Cohen, and R. Yagel. A Survey of Architectures for Volume Rendering. *IEEE Engineering in Medicine and Biology,* pp. 18–23, December 1990.

115. A. Kaufman, D. Cohen, and R. Yagel. Volume Graphics. *IEEE Computer,* 26(7):51–64, July 1993.

116. R.G. Keys. Cubic Convolution Interpolation for Digital Image Processing. *IEEE Transactions on Acoustics, Speech, and Signal Processing,* ASSP-29(6):1153–1160, December 1981.

117. J.T. Kajiya and B. Von Herzen. Ray Tracing Volume Densities. *Computer Graphics,* 18(3):165–174, July 1984.

118. U. Kanus, M. Meissner, W. Strasser, H. Pfister, and A. Kaufman. Cube-4 Implementations on the Teramac Custom Computing Machine. In *Proceedings of the 11th Workshop on Graphics Hardware,* Vol. EG96 HW, pp. 133–143. EuroGraphics Technical Report Series, Poitiers, France, August 1996.

119. J. Kaba, J. Matey, G. Stoll, and H. Taylor. Interactive Terrain Rendering and Volume Visualization on the Princeton Engine. In *Proceedings IEEE Visualization 92,* pp. 349–355. IEEE Computer Society Press, October 1992.

120. G. Knittel. Verve, Voxel Engine for Real-Time Visualization and Examination. In *Proceedings EuroGraphics '93,* pp. C37–C48. University Press, 1993.

121. G. Knittel. A VLSI Design for Fast Vector Normalization. In *Proceedings Eight EuroGraphics Workshop on Graphics Hardware,* Vol. EG93 HW, pp. 1–14. EuroGraphics Technical Report Series, 1993.

122. G. Knittel. A Scalable Architecture for Volume Rendering. In *Proceedings of the Ninth Workshop on Graphics Hardware,* Vol. EG94 HW, pp. 58–69. EuroGraphics Technical Report Series, Oslo, Norway, September 1994.

123. G. Knittel. A PCI-based Volume Rendering Accelerator. In *Proceedings of the Tenth Workshop on Graphics Hardware,* Vol. EG95 HW, pp. 73–82. EuroGraphics Technical Report Series, ISSN 1024-0861, Maastricht, The Netherlands, August 1995.

124. W. Krueger. Volume Rendering and Data Feature Enhancement. *Computer Graphics,* 24(5):21–26, November 1990.

125. W. Krueger. The Application of Transport Theory to Visualization of 3D Scalar Data Fields. *Computers in Physics,* 5(4):397–406, July/August 1991.

126. T.Y. Kong and J.K. Udupa. A Justification of a Fast Surface Trading Algorithm. *Computer Vision Graphics and Image Processing,* 54(2):162–170, March 1992.

127. Kubota. Volume Rendering with Denali. Technical report, Kubota Pacific Computer Inc., June 1993.

128. W.E. Lorensen and H.E. Cline. Marching Cubes: A High Resolution 3D Surface Construction Algorithm. *Computer Graphics,* 21(4):163–169, July 1987.

129. M.S. Levoy. Display of Surfaces from Volume Data. *IEEE Computer Graphics and Applications,* 5(3):29–37, May 1988.

130. M.S. Levoy. Design for a Real-Time High-Quality Volume Rendering Workstation. In *Proceedings of the Chapel Hill Workshop on Volume Visualization,* pp. 85–92, 1989.

131. M.S. Levoy. *Display of Surfaces from Volume Data.* Ph.D. thesis, University of North Carolina at Chapel Hill, 1989.

132. M.S. Levoy. Responds to Letter of the Editor. *IEEE Computer Graphics and Applications,* p. 91, March 1989.

133. M.S. Levoy. Efficient Ray Tracing of Volume Data. *ACM Transactions on Graphics,* 9(3):245–261, July 1990.

134. M.S. Levoy. A Hybrid Ray Tracer for Rendering Polygon and Volume Data. *IEEE Computer Graphics and Applications,* pp. 33–40, March 1990.

135. M.S. Levoy. Volume Rendering by Adaptive Refinement. *The Visual Computer,* 6(1):2–7, 1990.

136. M. Levoy. Volume Rendering Using the Fourier Projection-Slice Theorem. In *Proceedings of Graphic Interface '92,* Vol. 1992, pp. 61–69. Canadian Information Processing Society, 1992.

137. D. Laur and P. Hanrahan. Hierarchical Splatting: A Progressive Refinement Algorithm for Volume Rendering. *Computer Graphics,* 25(4):285–288, July 1991.

138. J. Lichtermann. Design of a Fast Voxel Processor for Parallel Volume Visualization. In *Proceedings of the Tenth Workshop on Graphics Hardware,* Vol. EG95 HW, pp. 83–92. EuroGraphics Technical Report Series, ISSN 1024-0861, Maastricht, The Netherlands, August 1995.

139. B. Lichtenbelt. Design of a High Performance Volume Visualization System. In *Proceedings 1997 SIGGRAPH/Eurographics Workshop on Graphics Hardware,* pp. 111–119. ACM SIGGRAPH, August 1997.

140. P. Lacroute and M. Levoy. Fast Volume Rendering Using a Shear-Warp Factorization of the Viewing Transformation. *Computer Graphics,* 28(4): 451–458, August 1994.

141. M.S. Levoy and R. Whitaker. Gaze-Directed Volume Rendering. *Computer Graphics,* 24(2):217–223, 1990.

142. C. Lee and C. Wood. A Modified Maximum Intensity Projection Display of MR Angiograms with Hybrid Order Interpolation. In *Proceedings of SPIE Medical Imaging 1995,* Vol. 2431. SPIE—The International Society for Optical Engineering, 1995.

143. A. Law, R. Yagel, and D.N. Jayasimha. VoxelFlow: A Parallel Volume Rendering Method for Scientific Visualization. In *Proceeding Int. Conf. on Computer Applications in Engineering and Medicine,* Indianapolis Indiana, March 1995, pp. 260–264

144. J. Marks, B. Andalman, P.A. Beardsley, W. Freeman, S. Gibson, J. Hodgins, T. Kang, B. Mirtich, H. Pfister, W. Ruml, K. Ryall, J. Seims, and S. Shieber. Design Galleries: A General Approach to Setting Parameters for Computer Graphics and Animation. In *Proceedings of SIGGRAPH '97,* pp. 389–400. ACM SIGGRAPH, New York, August 1997.

145. E. Maeland. On the Comparison of Interpolation Methods. *IEEE Transactions on Medical Imaging,* 7(3):213–217, September 1988.

146. T. Malzbender. Fourier Volume Rendering. *ACM Transaction on Graphics,* 12(3):233–250, July 1993.

147. David Marr. Theory of Edge Detection. In *Proceedings of the Royal Society, London,* Vol. B207, pp. 187–217, 1980.

148. N.L. Max. Optical Models for Direct Volume Rendering. *IEEE Transactions on Visualization and Computer Graphics,* 1(2):99–108, June 1995.

149. M. Margala, N.G. Durdle, S. Juskiw, V.J. Raso, and D.L. Hill. A 33MHz 16-Bit Gradient Calculator for Real-Time Volume Imaging. In *Proceedings 9th Eurographics Workshop on Graphics Hardware,* Vol. EG94 HW, pp. 80–85. EuroGraphics Technical Report Series ISSN 1017-4656, 1994.

150. D.J. Meagher. Efficient Synthetic Image Generation of Arbitrary 3D Objects. *Proceedings IEEE Computer Society Conference on Pattern Recognition and Image Processing,* pp. 473–478, June 1982.

151. D.J. Meagher. Applying Solids Processing Methods to Medical Planning. In *Proceedings of the National Computer Graphics Association,* pp. 101–109, 1985.

152. S. Molnar, J. Eyles, and J. Poulton. PixelFlow: High-Speed Rendering Using Image Composition. *Computer Graphics,* 26(2):231–240, July 1992.

153. N. Max, P. Hanrahan, and R. Crawfis. Area and Volume Coherence for Efficient Visualization of 3D Scalar Functions. *Computer Graphics,* 24(5): 27–33, November 1990.

154. S.R. Marschner and R.J. Lobb. An Evaluation of Reconstruction Filters for Volume Rendering. In *Proceedings IEEE Visualization 1994,* pp. 100–107. IEEE Computer Society Press, October 1994.

155. E. Maurincomme, I. Magnin, G. Finet, and R. Goutte. Methodology for Three-Dimensional Reconstruction of Intervascular Ultrasound Images. In *Proceedings SPIE Medical Imaging VI,* Vol. 1653, pp. 26–34. SPIE, 1992.

156. T. Moeller, R. Machiraju, K. Mueller, and R. Yagel. Classification and Local Error Estimation of Interpolation and Derivative Filters. *IEEE Symposium on Volume Visualization,* pp. 71–78, October 1996.

157. H.P. Meinzer, K. Meetz, D. Scheppelmann, U. Engelmann, and H.J. Baur. The Heidelberg Ray Tracing Model. *IEEE Computer Graphics and Applications,* pp. 34–43, November 1991.

158. D.P. Mitchell and A.N. Netravali. Reconstruction Filters in Computer Graphics. *Computer Graphics,* 22(4):221–228, August 1988.

159. S.E. Molnar. *Imaging-Composition Architectures for Real-Time Image Generation.* Ph.D. thesis, University of North Carolina at Chapel Hill, 1991.

160. K.L. Ma and J.S. Painter. Parallel Volume Visualization on Workstations. *Computers & Graphics,* 17(1):31–37, January/February 1993.

161. C. Montani and R. Scopigno. Rendering Volumetric Data using the STICKS Representation Scheme. *Computer Graphics,* 24(5):87–93, November 1990.

162. E.S. Manolakos, H.M. Stellakis, and D.H. Brooks. Parallel Processing for Biomedical Signal Processing. *Computer,* pp. 33–43, March 1991.

163. S. Muraki. Volume Data and Wavelet Transforms. *IEEE Computer Graphics and Applications,* 13(4):50–56, July 1993.

164. T. Malzbender, C. Wittenbrink, and M. Goss. Opacity-Weighted Color Interpolation for Volume Sampling. *HPLabs Technical Report,* (HPL-97-31), February 1997.

165. R. Machiraju and R. Yagel. Reconstruction Error Characterization and Control: A Sampling Theory Approach. *IEEE Transactions on Visualization and Computer Graphics,* 2(4):364–377, December 1996.

166. H. Neeman. A Decomposition Algorithm for Visualizing Irregular Grids. *Computer Graphics,* 24(5):49–56, November 1990.

167. U. Neumann. Interactive Volume Rendering on a Multicomputer. Technical Report, University of North Carolina at Chapel Hill, 1991.

168. U. Neumann. Interactive Volume Rendering on a Multicomputer. In *Proceedings of 1992 Symposium of Interactive 3D Graphics,* pp. 95–100, 1992.

169. U. Neumann. Parallel Volume-Rendering Algorithm Performance on Mesh-Connected Multicomputers. In *Proceedings of the 1993 Parallel Rendering Symposium,* pp. 97–104. ACM Press, 1993.

170. U. Neumann. *Volume Reconstruction and Parallel Rendering Algorithms: A Comparative Analysis:* Ph.D. thesis, University of North Carolina at Chapel Hill, 1993.

171. J. Nieh and M. Levoy. Volume Rendering on Scalable Sharde-Memory MIMD Architectures. In *Proceedings of the Boston Workshop on Volume Visualization,* pp. 17–24. ACM Press, 1992.

172. K.L. Novins, F.X. Sillion, and D.P. Greenberg. An Efficient Method for Volume Rendering Using Perspective Projection. *Computer Graphics,* 24(5):95–102, November 1991.

173. H.J. Noordmans, H.T.M. van der Voort, and A.W.M. Smeulders. Fast Volume Rendering for Interactive Usage. In *Proceedings of VIP '93,* pp. 137–140, 1993.

174. U. Neumann, T.S. Yoo, H. Fuchs and S.M. Pizer, T. Cullip, J. Rhoades, and R. Whitake. Achieving Direct Volume Visualization with Interactive Semantic Region Selection. Technical Report, University of North Carolina at Chapel Hill, 1991.

175. R. Ohbuchi, D. Chen, and H. Fuchs. Incremental Volume Reconstruction and Rendering for 3D Ultrasound Imaging. Technical Report, University of North Carolina at Chapel Hill, 1992.

176. R. Ohbuchi and H. Fuchs. Incremental Volume Rendering Algorithm for Interactive 3D Ultrasound Imaging. *Proceedings Information Processings in Medical Imaging,* pp. 486–500, 1991.

177. B. Olstad, E. Steen, and O. Sandsta. Shell Rendering with Hardware Supported Data Extraction. In *Proceedings of SPIE Medical Imaging 1995,* Vol. 2431. SPIE—The International Society for Optical Engineering, 1995.

178. T. Ohashi, T. Uchiki, and M. Tokoro. A Three-Dimensional Shaded Display Method for Voxel-Based Representation. In *Proceedings of Eurographics '85,* pp. 221–232, 1985.

179. James B. Pawley. *Handbook of Biological Confocal Microscopy.* Plenum Press, rev. ed., 1990. ISBN: 0-306-43538-1.

180. D.J. Plunkett and M.J. Bailey. The Vectorization of a Ray-Tracing Algorithm for Improved Executing Speed. *IEEE Computer Graphics and Application,* pp. 52–60, August 1985.

181. T. Porter and T. Duff. Compositing Digital Images. *Computer Graphics,* 18(3):253–259, July 1984.

182. B.T. Phong. Illumination for Computer Generated Pictures. *Communications of the ACM,* 18(6):311–317, June 1975.

183. K.P. Picott. Extentions of the Linear and Area Lighting Models. *IEEE Computer Graphics and Applications,* pp. 31–38, March 1992.

184. K.K. Pingle. Visual Perception by a Computer. In A. Grasselli, editor, *Automatic Interpretation and Classification of Images,* pp. 277–284. Academic Press, 1969.

185. H. Pfister and A. Kaufman. Real-Time Architecture for High Resolution Volume Visualization. In *Proceedings Eight Eurographics Workshop on Graphics Hardware,* Vol. EG93 HW, pp. 72–80. EuroGraphics Technical Report Series, 1993.

186. H. Pfister and A. Kaufman. Cube-4 a Scalable Architecture for Real-Time Volume Rendering. *IEEE Symposium on Volume Visualization,* pp. 47–54, October 1996.

187. J.A. Parker, R.V. Kenyon, and D.E. Troxel. Comparison of Interpolating Methods for Image Resampling. *IEEE Transactions on Medical Imaging,* 2(1):31–39, March 1983.

188. H. Pfister, A. Kaufman, and F. Wessels. Towards a Scalable Architecture for Real-Time Volume Rendering. In *Proceedings of the Tenth Workshop on Graphics Hardware,* Vol. EG95 HW, pp. 123–130. EuroGraphics Technical Report Series, ISSN 1024-0861, Maastricht, The Netherlands, August 1995.

189. H. Pfister, A. Kaufman, and W. Wessels. Towards a Scalable Architecture for Real-Time Volume Rendering. In *Proceedings of the Tenth Workshop on Graphics Hardware,* Vol. EG95 HW, pp. 123–130. EuroGraphics Technical Report Series, ISSN 1024-0861, Maastricht, The Netherlands, August 1995.

190. A. Pommert, B. Pflesser, M. Riemer, T. Schiemann, R. Schubert, U. Tiede, and K.H. Hohne. Advances in Medical Volume Visualization. In *State of the Art Report EuroGraphics '94,* Vol. EG94 STAR, pp. 111–139. EuroGraphics Technical Report Series ISSN 1017-4656, 1994.

191. S.K. Park and R.A. Schowengerdt. Image Reconstruction by Parametric Cubic Convolution. *Computer Vision, Graphics, and Image Processing,* 23(2):258–272, August 1983.

192. A. Pommert, U. Tiede, G. Wiebecke, and K.H. Hohne. Surface Shading in Tomographic Volume Visualization. In *Proceedings of the First Conference on Visualization in Biomedical Computing,* Vol. 1, pp. 19–26. IEEE Computer Society Press, 1990.

193. H. Pfister, F. Wessels, and A. Kaufman. Sheared Interpolation and Gradient Estimation for Real-Time Volume Rendering. In *Proceedings 9th Eurographics Workshop on Graphics Hardware,* Vol. EG94 HW, pp. 70–79. EuroGraphics Technical Report Series ISSN 1017-4656, 1994.

194. W.T. Reeves. Approximate and Probabilistic Algorithms for Shading and Rendering Structured Particle Systems. *Computer Graphics,* 19(3):313–322, July 1985.

195. R.A. Reynolds, D. Gordon, and Lih-Shyang Chen. A Dynamic Screen Technique for Shaded Graphics Display of Slice-Represented Objects. *Computer Vision, Graphics, and Image Processing,* 38(3):275–298, June 1987.

196. M. Rhodes. Computer Graphics in Medicine. *IEEE Computer Graphics and Applications,* pp. 20–23, March 1990.

197. M.L. Rhodes. Computer Graphics in Medicine: The Past Decade. *IEEE Computer Graphics and Applications,* pp. 52–54, January 1991.

198. M.L. Rhodes. Guest Editor's Introduction: Computer Graphics in Medicine. *IEEE Computer Graphics and Applications,* p. 27, November 1991.

199. R.A. Roberts and C.T. Mullis. *Digital Signal Processing.* Addison-Wesley, 1987.

200. R.A. Robb. Interactive Display and Analysis of 3D Medical Images. *IEEE Transactions on Medical Imaging,* 8(3):217–226, September 1989.

201. L.R. Rabiner and R.W. Schafer. On the Behavior of Minimax Relative Error FIR Digital Differentiators. *The Bell System Technical Journal,* 53(2): 333–347, February 1974.

202. L.R. Rabiner and R.W. Schafer. On the Behavior of Minimax Relative Error FIR Digital Differentiators. *The Bell System Technical Journal,* 53(2): 333–361, February 1974.

203. S.P. Raya and J.K. Udupa. Shape-Based Interpolation of Multidimensional Objects. *IEEE Transactions on Medical Imaging,* 9(1):32–42, 1990.

204. S.P. Raya, J.K. Udupa, and W.A. Barrett. A PC-Based 3D Imaging System: Algorithms, Software, and Hardware Considerations. *Computerized Medical Imaging and Graphics,* 14(5):353–370, September-October 1990.

205. S.M. Rubin and T. Whitted. A 3-Dimensional Representation for Fast Rendering of Complex Scenes. *Computer Graphics,* 14(3):110–116, July 1980.

206. P. Sabella. A Rendering Algorithm for Visualizing 3D Scalar Fields. *Computer Graphics,* 22(4):51–58, August 1988.

207. J. Smit and M.J. Bentum. Visualization of 3D Datasets in Real-Time. In *Proceedings VIP '93,* pp. 71–73, 1993.

208. J. Smit, M.J. Bentum, M.M. Samsom, and H. Snijders. A Plane Interpolator for 3D Visualization Applications in Real-Time. In *Proceedings of the IEEE ProRisc Conference,* pp. 165–167, 1993.

209. J. Smit, M.J. Bentum, A. van der Horst, and H.J. Wessels. On the Design of a Real-Time Volume Rendering Engine. In *Proceedings of the Seventh Workshop on Graphics Hardware,* Vol. EG92 HW, pp. 70–76. EuroGraphics Technical Report Series, 1992.

210. L. Sobierajski, D. Cohen, R. Yagel, A. Kaufman, and D. Acker. Fast Display Method for Volumetric Data. *The Visual Computer,* 10(2):116–124, 1993.

211. M.R. Stytz, G. Frieder, and O. Frieder. Three-Dimensional Medical Imaging: Algorithms and Computer Systems. *ACM Computer Surveys,* 23(4): 421–499, December 1991.

212. A. Sunguroff and D. Greenberg. Computer Generated Images for Medical Applications. *Computer Graphics,* 12(3):196–202, August 1978.

213. J.P. Singh, A. Gupta, and M. Levoy. Parallel Visualization Algorithms: Performance and Architectural Implications. Technical report, Stanford University, 1994.

214. C. Silva, L. Hong, and A. Kaufman. Flow Surface Probes for Vector Field Visualization. Technical Report, State University of New York at Stony Brook, 1994.

215. C. Silva. Parallel Processing for Volume Visualization. Technical Report, State University of New York at Stony Brook, October 1992.

216. D. Speray and S. Kennon. Volume Probes: Interactive Data Exploration on Arbitrary Grids. *Computer Graphics,* 24(5):5–12, November 1990.

217. R. Shu and M.S. Kankanhalli. Generating a Linear Octree from Voxel Data for a Connected Object. In *Proceedings SPIE Medical Imaging VI*, Vol. 1653, pp. 17–25. SPIE, 1992.

218. C.T. Silva and A.E. Kaufman. Parallel Performance Measures for Volume Ray Casting. In *Proceedings IEEE Visualization 94*. IEEE Computer Society Press, 1994.

219. P. Shirley and H. Neeman. Volume Visualization at the Center for Super-computing Research and Development. In *Proceedings of the Chapel Hill Workshop on Volume Visualization*, pp. 17–20, 1989.

220. E. Steen and B. Olstad. Volume Rendering of 3D Medical Ultrasound Data Using Direct Feature Mapping. *IEEE Transaction on Medical Imaging*, 13(3):517–525, September 1994.

221. L.M. Sobierajski. *Global Illumination Models for Volume Rendering*. Ph.D. thesis, State University of New York at Stony Brook, August 1994.

222. I. Sobel. An Isotropic $3 \times 3 \times 3$ Volume Gradient Operator. Technical Report, Hewlett-Packard Laboratories, April 1995.

223. J. Smit, R. Peer, and M.J. Bentum. A Composition Unit for 3D Visualization in Real-Time. In *Proceedings of the IEEE ProRisc Conference*, pp. 169–170, 1993.

224. P. Sprawls. *Physical Principles of Medical Imaging*. Medical Physics Publishing, Madison, Wisconsin, 2nd ed., 1995. ISBN:0-944838-54-5.

225. P. Schroeder and J. Salem. Fast Rotation of Volume Data on Data Parallel Architectures. In *Proceedings IEEE Visualization 91*, pp. 50–57. IEEE Computer Society Press, 1991.

226. P. Schroeder and G. Stoll. Data Parallel Volume Rendering as Line Drawing. In *Proceedings of the Boston Workshop on Volume Visualization*, pp. 25–32. ACM Press, 1992.

227. T. Saito and T. Takahashi. Comprehensible Rendering of 3D Shapes. *Computer Graphics*, 24(4):197–206, August 1990.

228. P. Shirley and A. Tuchman. A Polygonal Approximation to Direct Scalar Volume Rendering. *Computer Graphics*, 24(5):63–70, November 1990.

229. H. Samet and R.E. Webber. Hierarchical Data Structures and Algorithms for Computer Graphics: Part II: Applications. *IEEE Computer Graphics and Applications*, pp. 59–75, July 1988.

230. J. Smit, H.J. Wessels, A. van der Horst, and M.J. Bentum. On the Design of a Real-Time Volume Rendering Engine. *Computer and Graphics*, 19(2):297–300, 1995.

231. U. Tiede, K.H. Hoehne, M. Bomans, A. Pommert, M. Riemer, and G. Wiebecke. Investigations of Medical 3D-Rendering Algorithms. *IEEE Computer Graphics and Applications*, pp. 41–53, March 1990.

232. T. Totsuka and M. Levoy. Frequency Domain Volume Rendering. In *Proceedings Siggraph 1993*, pp. 271–278, August 1993.

233. H.K. Tuy and L.T. Tuy. Direct 2-D Display of 3-D Objects. *IEEE Computer Graphics and Applications*, pp. 29–33, November 1984.

234. J.K. Udupa and V.G. Ajjanagadde. Boundary and Object Labelling in Three-Dimensional Images. *Computer Vision Graphics and Image Processing*, 51:355–369, 1990.

235. J.K. Udupa and R.J. Goncalves. Imaging Transforms for Surface and Volume Rendering. Technical Report, University of Pennsylvania, Department of Radiology, January 1992.

236. J.K. Udupa and G.T. Herman. Volume Rendering versus Surface Rendering, a Technical Correspondence. *Communications of the ACM*, 32(11):1364–1367, November 1989.

237. J.K. Udupa and H.M. Hung. Surface versus Volume Rendering: A Comparative Assessment. Technical report, University of Pennsylvania, Department of Radiology, March 1990.

238. J.K. Udupa, H.M. Hung, and K. Chuang. Surface and Volume Rendering in 3D Imaging: A Comparison. *Journal of Digital Imaging*, 4(3):159–168, August 1991.

239. J.K. Udupa, H.M. Hung, D. Odhner, and R. Goncalves. Multidimensional Data Format Specification: A Generalization of the American College of Radiology—National Electric Manufactures Association Standards. *Journal of Digital Imaging*, 5(1):26–45, February 1992.

240. C. Upson and M. Keeler. V-Buffer: Visible Volume Rendering. *Computer Graphics*, 22(4):59–64, August 1988.

241. J.K. Udupa and D. Odhner. Fast Visualization, Manipulation, and Analysis of Binary Volumetric Objects. *IEEE Computer Graphics and Applications*, pp. 53–62, November 1991.

242. J.K. Udupa and D. Odhner. Shell Rendering: Fast Volume Rendering and Analysis of Fuzzy Surfaces. In *Proceedings SPIE Medical Imaging VI*, Vol. 1653, pp. 35–43. SPIE, 1992.

243. J.K. Udupa and D. Odhner. Shell Rendering: Fast Volume Rendering and Analysis of Fuzzy Surfaces. Technical report, University of Pennsylvania, Department of Radiology, January 1992.

244. J.K. Udupa and D. Odhner. Shell Rendering. *IEEE Computer Graphics and Applications*, 13(6):58–67, November 1993.

245. H.T.M. van der Voort, J.M. Messerli, H.J. Noordmans, and A.W.M. Smeulders. Volume Visualization for Interactive Microscopic Image Analysis. *Bioimaging*, 1(1):20–29, March 1993.

246. M.W. Vannier, T. Pilgram, G. Bhatia, and B. Brunsden. Facial Surface Scanner. *IEEE Computer Graphics and Applications*, pp. 72–80, November 1991.

247. A. Wallin. Constructing Isosurfaces from CT Data. *IEEE Computer Graphics and Applications*, pp. 28–33, November 1991.

248. J. Ward and D.R. Cok. Resampling Algorithms for Image Resizing and Rotation. In *SPIE Digital Image Processing Applications*, Vol. 1075, pp. 197–226, 1989.

249. J. Williams, J. Challinger, N. Alper, and S. Ramamoorthy. Direct Volume Rendering of Curvilinear Volumes. *Computer Graphics*, 24(5):41–47, November 1990.

250. Lee Westover. Interactive Volume Rendering. In *Chapel Hill Workshop on Volume Visualization*, pp. 9–16, May 1989.

251. L. Westover. Footprints Evaluation for Volume Rendering. *Computer Graphics*, 24(4):367–376, August 1990.

252. S. Whitman. *Multiprocessor Methods for Computer Graphics.* Jones and Bartlett, 1992.

253. J. Wilhelms. Decisions in Volume Rendering. *SIGGRAPH '91 Course Notes 8-State of the Art in Volume Visualization,* pp. I.1–I.11, July 1991.

254. S. Wang and A. Kaufman. Volume Sampled Voxelization of Geometric Primitives. In *Proceedings IEEE Visualization 1993,* pp. 78–84. IEEE Computer Society Press, October 1993.

255. R.H. Wolfe and C.N. Liu. Interactive Visualization of 3D Seismic Data: A Volumetric Method. *IEEE Computer Graphics and Application,* pp. 24–30, July 1988.

256. J.W. Wallis, T.R. Miller, C.A. Lerner, and E.C. Kleerup. Three-Dimensional Display in Nuclear Medicine. *IEEE Transactions on Medical Imaging,* 8(4):297–303, December 1989.

257. G. Wolberg. *Digital Image Warping.* IEEE Computer Society Press, 3rd ed., 1994. ISBN: 0-8186-8944-7.

258. J. Wilhelms and A. van Gelder. Octrees for Faster Isosurface Generation Extended Abstract. *Computer Graphics,* 24(5):57–62, November 1990.

259. J. Wilhelms and A. van Gelder. Topological Considerations in Isosurface Generation Extended Abstract. *Computer Graphics,* 24(5):79–86, November 1990.

260. J. Wilhelms and A. van Gelder. A Coherent Projection Approach for Direct Volume Rendering. *Computer Graphics,* 25(4):275–284, July 1991.

261. J. Wilhelms and A. van Gelder. Octrees for Faster Isosurface Generation. *ACM Transactions on Graphics,* 11(3):201–227, 1992.

262. J. Wilhelms and A. van Gelder. Multidimensional Trees for Controlled Volume Rendering and Compression. *IEEE/ACM Symposium on Volume Visualization,* pp. 27–34, October 1994.

263. R. Yagel. Realistic Display of Volumes. In *Proceedings of Medical Imaging VI: Image Capture, Formatting, and Display,* Vol. 1653, pp. 470–476. SPIE, 1991.

264. R. Yagel, D. Cohen, and A. Kaufman. Discrete Ray Tracing. *Computer Graphics and Applications,* 12(5):19–28, September 1992.

265. R. Yagel, D. Cohen, and A. Kaufman. Normal Estimation in 3D Discrete Space. *The Visual Computer,* 8(5-6):278–291, June 1992.

266. J. Yla-Jaaski, F. Klein, and O. Kubler. Fast Direct Display of Volume Data for Medical Diagnosis. *Computer Vision, Graphics and Image Processing: Graphical Models and Image Processing,* 53(1):7–18, January 1991.

267. R. Yagel and A. Kaufman. Template-Based Volume Viewing. *Computer Graphics Forum,* 11(3):153–167, September 1992.

268. B.L. Yeo and B. Liu. Volume Rendering of DCT-Based Compressed 3D Scalar Data. *IEEE Transactions on Visualization and Computer Graphics,* 1(1):29–43, March 1995.

269. T.S. Yoo, U. Neumann, H. Fuchs, S.M. Pizer, T. Cullip, J. Rhoades, and R. Whitaker. Direct Visualization of Volume Data. *IEEE Computer Graphics and Applications,* 12(4):63–71, July 1992.

270. S.W. Zucker and R.A. Hummel. A Three-Dimensional Edge Operator. *IEEE Transactions on Pattern Analysis and Machine Intelligence,* 3(3):324–331, May 1981.

271. K.J. Zuiderveld, A.H.J. Koning, and M.A. Viergever. Acceleration of Ray-casting Using 3D Distance Transforms. In *SPIE Proceedings Visualization in Biomedical Computing,* Vol. 1808, pp. 324–335, 1992.

272. K.J. Zuiderveld. *Visualization of Multimodality Medical Volume Data using Object-Oriented Methods.* Ph.D. thesis, University of Utrecht, March 1995.

273. J.C. Russ. *The Image Processing Handbook,* Second Edition. CRC Press, ISBN 0-8493-2516-1, 1995.

INDEX

A

B

C

I

L

M

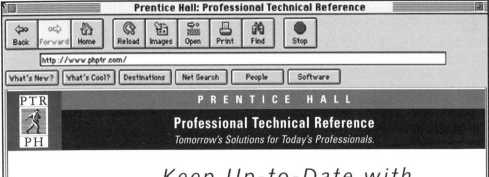

8.   **LIMITED WARRANTY AND DISCLAIMER OF WARRANTY:** The Company warrants that the SOFTWARE, when properly used in accordance with the Documentation, will operate in substantial conformity with the description of the SOFTWARE set forth in the Documentation. The Company does not warrant that the SOFTWARE will meet your requirements or that the operation of the SOFTWARE will be uninterrupted or error-free. The Company warrants that the media on which the SOFTWARE is delivered shall be free from defects in materials and workmanship under normal use for a period of thirty (30) days from the date of your purchase. Your only remedy and the Company's only obligation under these limited warranties is, at the Company's option, return of the warranted item for a refund of any amounts paid by you or replacement of the item. Any replacement of SOFTWARE or media under the warranties shall not extend the original warranty period. The limited warranty set forth above shall not apply to any SOFTWARE which the Company determines in good faith has been subject to misuse, neglect, improper installation, repair, alteration, or damage by you. EXCEPT FOR THE EXPRESSED WARRANTIES SET FORTH ABOVE, THE COMPANY DISCLAIMS ALL WARRANTIES, EXPRESS OR IMPLIED, INCLUDING WITHOUT LIMITATION, THE IMPLIED WARRANTIES OF MERCHANTABILITY AND FITNESS FOR A PARTICULAR PURPOSE. EXCEPT FOR THE EXPRESS WARRANTY SET FORTH ABOVE, THE COMPANY DOES NOT WARRANT, GUARANTEE, OR MAKE ANY REPRESENTATION REGARDING THE USE OR THE RESULTS OF THE USE OF THE SOFTWARE IN TERMS OF ITS CORRECTNESS, ACCURACY, RELIABILITY, CURRENTNESS, OR OTHERWISE.

IN NO EVENT, SHALL THE COMPANY OR ITS EMPLOYEES, AGENTS, SUPPLIERS, OR CONTRACTORS BE LIABLE FOR ANY INCIDENTAL, INDIRECT, SPECIAL, OR CONSEQUENTIAL DAMAGES ARISING OUT OF OR IN CONNECTION WITH THE LICENSE GRANTED UNDER THIS AGREEMENT, OR FOR LOSS OF USE, LOSS OF DATA, LOSS OF INCOME OR PROFIT, OR OTHER LOSSES, SUSTAINED AS A RESULT OF INJURY TO ANY PERSON, OR LOSS OF OR DAMAGE TO PROPERTY, OR CLAIMS OF THIRD PARTIES, EVEN IF THE COMPANY OR AN AUTHORIZED REPRESENTATIVE OF THE COMPANY HAS BEEN ADVISED OF THE POSSIBILITY OF SUCH DAMAGES. IN NO EVENT SHALL LIABILITY OF THE COMPANY FOR DAMAGES WITH RESPECT TO THE SOFTWARE EXCEED THE AMOUNTS ACTUALLY PAID BY YOU, IF ANY, FOR THE SOFTWARE.

SOME JURISDICTIONS DO NOT ALLOW THE LIMITATION OF IMPLIED WARRANTIES OR LIABILITY FOR INCIDENTAL, INDIRECT, SPECIAL, OR CONSEQUENTIAL DAMAGES, SO THE ABOVE LIMITATIONS MAY NOT ALWAYS APPLY. THE WARRANTIES IN THIS AGREEMENT GIVE YOU SPECIFIC LEGAL RIGHTS AND YOU MAY ALSO HAVE OTHER RIGHTS WHICH VARY IN ACCORDANCE WITH LOCAL LAW.

ACKNOWLEDGMENT

YOU ACKNOWLEDGE THAT YOU HAVE READ THIS AGREEMENT, UNDERSTAND IT, AND AGREE TO BE BOUND BY ITS TERMS AND CONDITIONS. YOU ALSO AGREE THAT THIS AGREEMENT IS THE COMPLETE AND EXCLUSIVE STATEMENT OF THE AGREEMENT BETWEEN YOU AND THE COMPANY AND SUPERSEDES ALL PROPOSALS OR PRIOR AGREEMENTS, ORAL, OR WRITTEN, AND ANY OTHER COMMUNICATIONS BETWEEN YOU AND THE COMPANY OR ANY REPRESENTATIVE OF THE COMPANY RELATING TO THE SUBJECT MATTER OF THIS AGREEMENT.

Should you have any questions concerning this Agreement or if you wish to contact the Company for any reason, please contact in writing at the address below.

Robin Short
Prentice Hall PTR
One Lake Street
Upper Saddle River, New Jersey 07458

About the CD-ROM

The CD-ROM packaged with this book contains the following:

1. Eleven high-quality volumetric data sets of varying sizes, from different sources. It is our hope that these data sets will stimulate experimentation with volume rendering.

2. Complete C source code that will take you step-by-step through the whole volume rendering pipeline. We show how matrix manipulations and transformations work. We take you through how to implement a simple Maximum Intensity Projection renderer all the way through to gradient calculation, shading, and classification as well as front-to-back compositing. If you don't have a C compiler, do not worry. We have included pre-compiled executables as well. You can find the source code in the directory D:\source. More information can be found in the readme.txt files in each directory.

3. An HTML file with interesting World Wide Web sites relating to volume rendering. Open the file D:\index.htm with your favorite browser.

All the pre-compiled executables can be run from the CD directly. If you want to experiment with the source code and compile it yourself, copy the directory structure D:\source\ to your harddisk. We assumed that D: is your CD-ROM drive.

For more information on the CD contents, please read the readme.txt files which you will find in almost all the directories.

Platform/System Requirements
Software on this CD-ROM requires Windows 95, Windows NT or higher.

Technical Support: Prentice Hall does not offer technical support for this software. However, if there is a problem with the media, you may obtain a replacement copy by e-mailing us with your problem at: *ptr_techsupport @phptr.com.*